INTERNATIONAL REMITTANCES

BACKGROUND, VERIFICATION PROPOSALS AND MONEY LAUNDERING ISSUES

MONETARY, FISCAL AND TRADE POLICIES

Additional books in this series can be found on Nova's website under the Series tab.

Additional e-books in this series can be found on Nova's website under the eBooks tab.

MONETARY, FISCAL AND TRADE POLICIES

INTERNATIONAL REMITTANCES

BACKGROUND, VERIFICATION PROPOSALS AND MONEY LAUNDERING ISSUES

CAMERON SLATON
EDITOR

New York

Library of Congress Cataloging-in-Publication Data

ISBN: 978-1-53610-158-4

Published by Nova Science Publishers, Inc. † New York

CONTENTS

PREFACE

This book focuses on remittances, transfers of money and capital sent by migrants and foreign immigrant communities to their home country. At over $432 billion in 2015, remittances sent home by international migrants to developing countries is larger than official development assistance (ODA) and more stable than private capital flows to these countries. The United States is the largest destination for international migrants and by far the largest source of global remittances. The World Bank estimates $56.3 billion in official remittance outflows from the United States in 2014. As the market for remittances has ballooned, banks, traditional money transfer companies, and entrepreneurs have responded to increased demand by increasing the amount of remittance channels available to migrants, including mobile, Internet, and card-based options. This book also examines the potential effects of a fine on remitters unable to provide proof of legal immigration status; the Bureau of Economic Analysis' (BEA) remittance estimate and the extent to which its revised estimation methodology met government-wide policies and best practices; the Bank Secrecy Act (BSA) remittance requirements that exist for remittance providers and related challenges that remittance providers face in complying with these requirements; money laundering risks that remittances pose; and stakeholders' views on the extent to which requiring remittance providers to verify identification and collect information at a lower dollar transaction amount than is currently required, or adding a requirement to verify legal immigration status, would assist federal agencies' anti-money laundering (AML) efforts.

In: International Remittances
Editor: Cameron Slaton

ISBN: 978-1-53610-158-4

Chapter 1

REMITTANCES: BACKGROUND AND ISSUES FOR CONGRESS*

Martin A. Weiss

SUMMARY

This report focuses on remittances, transfers of money and capital sent by migrants and foreign immigrant communities to their home country. At over $432 billion in 2015, remittances sent home by international migrants to developing countries is larger than official development assistance (ODA) and more stable than private capital flows to these countries.

The United States is the largest destination for international migrants and by far the largest source of global remittances. The World Bank estimates $56.3 billion in official remittance outflows from the United States in 2014. As the market for remittances has ballooned, banks, traditional money transfer companies, and entrepreneurs have responded to increased demand by increasing the amount of remittance channels available to migrants, including mobile, Internet, and card-based options.

The dramatic rise in the importance of remittances to global capital flows has led Congress and other policymakers to take a greater interest in these flows. Key issues for Congress include:

Regulation of Remittances. Members may want to review the regulatory landscape for remittance providers. Effective and proportional

* This is an edited, reformatted and augmented version of a Congressional Research Service, Publication No. R43217, dated May 9, 2016.

regulation of remittances reduces corruption, enhances transparency, and facilitates a more robust business environment. At the same time, additional regulatory requirements, such as recent consumer protection requirements included in the *Dodd-Frank Wall Street Consumer Protection Act*, may raise concerns about the compliance costs for remittance providers and consumers.

Congress may also want to consider whether current federal and state regulation are appropriate for new and emerging payments systems such as mobile and card options, which are starting to capture part of the remittance market. Members may also want to review recent efforts to improve foreign regulatory and supervisory mechanisms. Remittances are often sent to recipients in developing countries with weak regulatory systems, increasing the risk of money laundering and possible financing of terrorism.

Impact on U.S. Development Policy. Remittances represent a substantial percentage of gross domestic product (GDP) in several developing countries. Whether remittances can be leveraged to support U.S. foreign development policy is another issue of concern to some Members of Congress. Some analysts argue that since remittances are comprised of private transfers between family members and friends, U.S. efforts should be directed to reducing the transaction costs involved in remittance transactions. Others note the potential beneficial development aspects of remittances, including promoting investment and access to financial services, and encouraging government programs to help stimulate these positive effects.

Remittances and U.S. Immigration Policy. Members may want to consider the interplay of U.S. remittance policy and U.S. immigration policy. A major goal of U.S. policy on remittances is increasing the attractiveness of regulated remittance systems to potential remittance customers, without regard to their legal status. Thus, U.S. Treasury officials allow remittance providers to accept certain foreign-issued means of identification to meet their customer identification requirements. Some Members argue that policies like these may undermine U.S. immigration laws and advocate restricting remittances to those with legal status under U.S. immigration laws. Others argue that more restrictive identification measures would only push remittance flows toward high-risk, unregulated and underground channels.

INTRODUCTION

This report focuses on remittances, transfers of money and capital sent by migrants and foreign immigrant communities to their home county. Increasing migration is a defining feature of the current global economy. Migrants account for around 3.4% of the global population[1] and the number of foreign-born residents in the United States is at its highest level in U.S. history, reaching 42.4 million in 2014.[2] Foreign-born residents of the United States made up 13.3% of the U.S. population in 2010, approaching levels not seen since 1910 (14.8%).[3] Foreign migrants and their communities in the United States sent $56.3 billion in 2014, around 13% of total worldwide sent in 2014.[4]

As migrants have become increasingly integrated into the global economy, their involvement in the economic activities of their home countries has also increased.[5] In 2015, worldwide remittance flows are estimated to have exceeded $601 billion. Of that amount, developing countries are estimated to receive about $432 billion, nearly three times the amount of official development assistance (ODA).[6] Only foreign direct investment (FDI) is a larger source of foreign capital for the world's developing countries than remittances.[7]

The dramatic rise in the importance of remittances to global capital flows has led Congress and other policymakers to take a greater interest in these flows and how they are covered under U.S. and state regulation. Recent financial reform legislation, for example, P.L. 111-203, the *Dodd-Frank Wall Street Reform and Consumer Protection Act*, provided federal consumer protections on remittance transactions. Remittances are also subject to federal regulation to prevent money laundering and terrorist financing.

This report provides general background on remittances, analyzes global and U.S. remittance flows, examines the remittance marketplace and the regulatory regime for sending remittances from the United States, and discusses key issues for Congress.

BACKGROUND

Remittances are cross-border migrant financial transfers. The primary source for international remittances data is the International Monetary Fund (IMF), which compiles statistics submitted by its member countries. Using IMF statistics, the World Bank publishes an annual *Migration and Remittances Factbook,* and monthly and annual remittances data on its website.[8] There are ongoing efforts to improve remittance data.

Remittances are currently defined as the sum of three entries in the IMF's annual Balance of Payments Statistics Yearbook: workers remittances; compensation of employees; and migrants' transfers.[9]

- **Workers' remittances** are defined by the IMF as transfers (cash or in kind) by migrants who are employed and considered resident in another country. If the migrants live in the host country for one year or longer, they are considered residents, regardless of their immigration status.
- **Compensation of employees** includes wages, salaries, and other benefits of border, seasonal, and other nonresident workers (such as local staff of embassies) away from their home country for less than a year.
- **Migrants' transfers** are the net worth of migrants' assets that are transfers from one country to another at the time of migration (for a period of at least one year), such as in the case of temporary workers.

A remittance transaction typically involves a sender, a recipient, intermediaries in both countries, and a payment system used by the intermediaries (**Figure 1**).[10] Remittances can be sent through informal or formal channels. Informal channels have been labeled by various terms, including "alternative remittance systems," "underground banks," and "informal value transfer systems." The most well-known is *hawala* (hawala means "transfer" in Arabic), which originated in India and has been in use in South Asia and the Middle East for several hundred years.[11] These services are less expensive than formal banking or money transfer arrangements, can provide anonymity for all parties involved, and can reach countries where there is no formal banking sector, in some cases even arranging for hand delivery of the cash. While most use these systems for legitimate purposes, their lack of documentation and anonymous, informal nature may make them attractive for money laundering and/or terrorist financing purposes.

Formal channels involve intermediaries that are officially licensed to operate money transfer businesses. These consist of banks, non-bank financial institutions, such as credit unions, savings and loan institutions, and post-offices, and money service businesses such as Western Union or MoneyGram. Increased use of technology in developing countries has also facilitated the use of mobile and other alternative payment options.

The price of sending a remittance can vary significantly. A number of factors affect the transfer fee charged, including the regulatory and administrative costs, the volume sent, the transfer mechanism, the receiving country's financial infrastructure, and the level of market competition (in both the sending and receiving country). In addition, the exchange rate used in the transaction can significantly affect the amount actually delivered to the recipient.

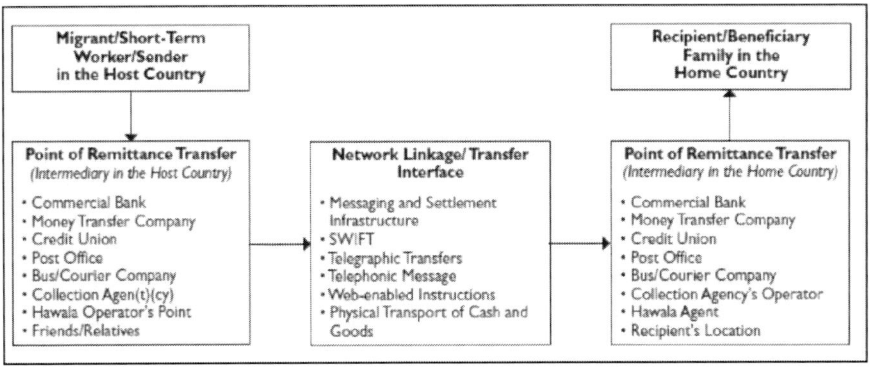

Source: International Transactions in Remittances: Guide for Compilers and Users, *International Monetary Fund*, 2009.

Notes: Not all transactions sent through these channels are remittances.

Figure 1. Overview of Remittance Channels.

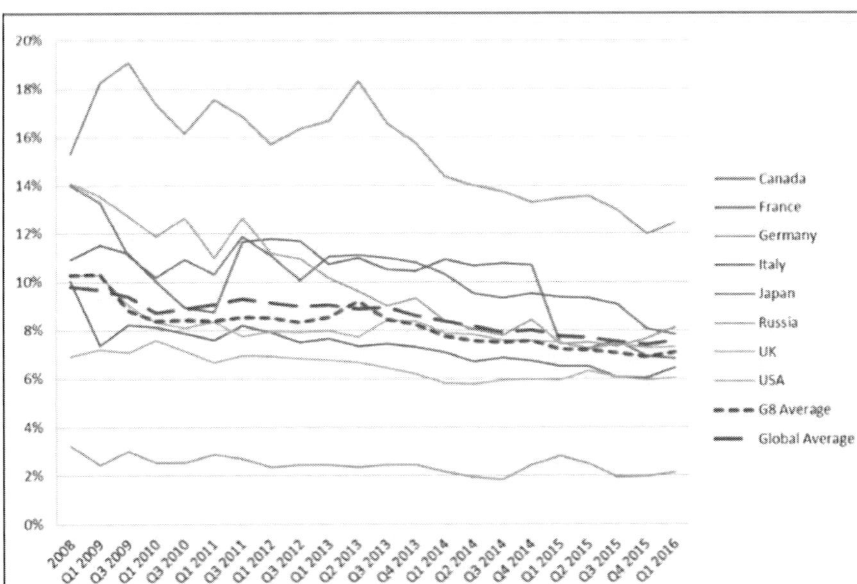

Source: Remittance Prices Worldwide, the World Bank

Figure 2. Total Average Cost of Sending Remittances from G8 Countries.

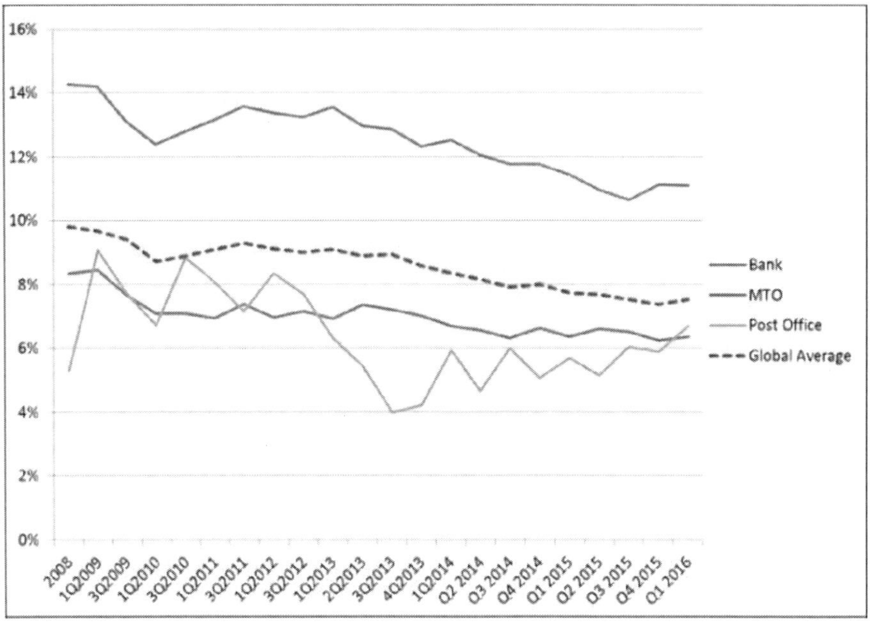

Source: Remittance Prices Worldwide, the World Bank.

Figure 3. Total Cost to Send Remittances by Service Provider.

For the most part, the cost of sending remittances has declined slightly in recent years, but substantial progress would need to be made to meet the G8 target of 5% of total cost set in 2009. According to World Bank analysis, the global average remittance cost has declined from 9.81% of the total transaction in 2008 to 7.53% during the first quarter of 2016.[12] Among the major economies, the United States is among the least costly from which to send money (Figure 2). For the first quarter of 2016, the average cost to send a remittance from the United States was 6.04% of the transaction.[13] The World Bank also tracks the cost of sending remittances from the main remittance providers. Recent data shows that banks continue to be the most expensive providers, followed by post offices. Money Transfer Operators (MTOs) such as Western Union and Moneygram are the cheapest (Figure 3).

Global and U.S Remittance Flows

Remittances have increased steadily over the past three decades. In 1990, remittances to developing countries totaled about $75 billion. At the time, remittances were a larger source of foreign capital to developing countries than both foreign direct investment and private capital flows (debt and equity). According to the World Bank, remittances to developing countries are estimated to have risen to $432 billion in 2015. Official remittance figures do not include informal remittance flows, which may account for an additional 35% to 75% of total remittance flows.[14] In 2015, India was the largest remittance-receiving country ($69 billion), followed by China ($64 billion), and the Philippines ($28 billion). **Figure 5** shows the geographical distribution of remittances since 2000.

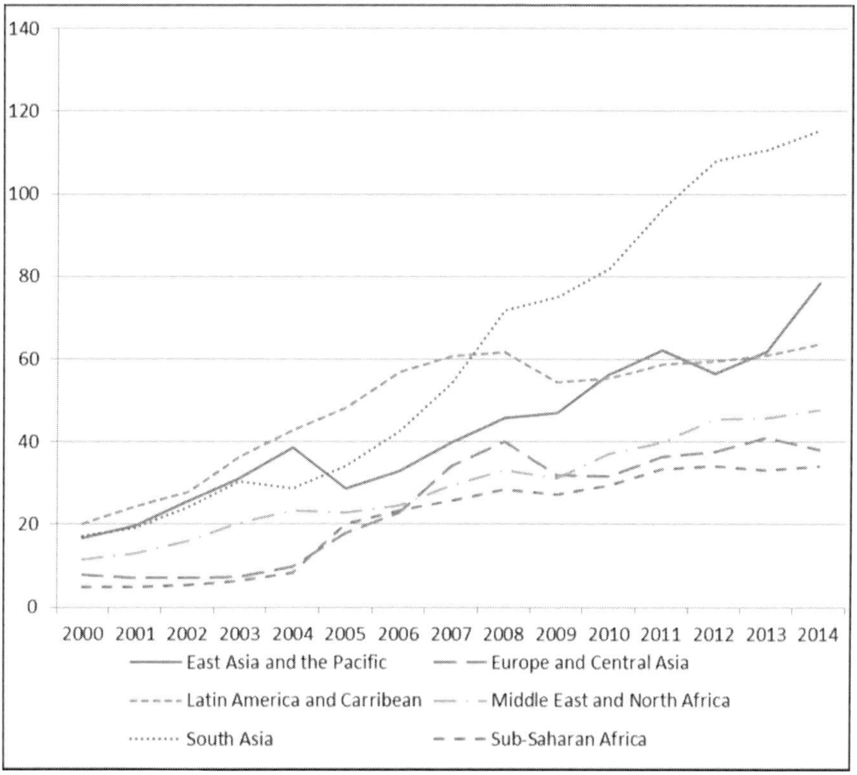

Source: World Bank, World Development Indicators.

Figure 4. Remittances to Developing Countries, by Region, 2000-2014; In Billions of U.S. Dollars.

Table 1. Largest Recipients of Remittance (Highlighted countries are on both lists)

	Billions of USD (2015)		Percentage of GDP (2014 unless otherwise indicated)
India	$68.91	Tajikistan	41.7%
China	$63.94	Kyrgyz Republic	30.3%
Philippines	$28.48	Nepal	9.7%
Mexico	$24.79	Tonga	26.3%
France	$22.98	Moldova	26.1%
Nigeria	$20.66	Liberia	23.2%
Egypt, Arab Rep.	$19.71	Haiti	22.4%
Pakistan	$19.25	Gambia, The	21.2%
Bangladesh	$15.36	Comoros	20.2%
Germany	$15.09	Lesotho	18.3%
Vietnam	$13.20	Armenia	17.8%
Spain	$10.24	Samoa	17.5%
Indonesia	$9.63	Honduras	17.4%
Italy	$9.58	El Salvador	16.8%
Belgium	$8.84	Lebanon	16.3%
Lebanon	$7.16	Jamaica	16.3%
Russian Federation	$7.10	Kosovo	15.7%
United States	$7.09	West Bank and Gaza	15.6%
Sri Lanka	$7.00	Marshall Islands	12.6%
Nepal	$6.98	Georgia	12.0%
Poland	$6.90	Bosnia and Herzegovina	11.1%
Guatemala	$6.61	Guyana	10.6%
Korea, Rep.	$6.54	Jordan	10.3%
Morocco	$6.42	Senegal	10.3%
Ukraine	$5.99	Cabo Verde	10.1%
United Kingdom	$5.49	Philippines	10.0%
Thailand	$5.22	Guatemala	9.9%
Dominican Republic	$5.15	Nicaragua	9.7%
Colombia	$4.64	Montenegro	9.4%
Japan	$4.48	Uzbekistan	9.0%
El Salvador	$4.36	Sri Lanka	8.9%

	Billions of USD (2015)		Percentage of GDP (2014 unless otherwise indicated)
Hungary	$4.20	Bangladesh	8.7%
Portugal	$4.09	Albania	8.6%
Jordan	$3.79	Sao Tome and Principe	8.6%
Honduras	$3.73	Serbia	8.4%
Myanmar	$3.47	Kiribati	7.7%
Yemen, Rep.	$3.41	Togo	7.6%
Serbia	$3.36	Dominican Republic	7.5%
Romania	$3.21	Mali	7.4%
Sweden	$3.18	Pakistan	7.0%

The emergence of large Indian, Chinese, and Philippine diaspora populations led to the explosive growth of remittances over the past 15 years. Between 2000 and 2014, remittances to developing countries in East Asia and Pacific increased by 370%, growing from $17 billion in 2000 to $79 billion in 2014. In South Asia, remittances increased by 571% over the time period, growing from $17 billion in 2000 to $116 billion in 2014. Despite accounting for a much smaller amount of global remittances, flows to Sub-Saharan Africa increased by 608% from 2000 ($5 billion) to 2014 ($34 billion).

Table 1 presents the 40 largest recipients of remittances ranked by the total amount of remittances received and by the percentage share of GDP. India is the largest individual recipient of remittances followed by China, Philippines, and Mexico. While remittances serve as an important component of a diversified mix of external finance in emerging market and middle-income countries, for the poorest countries, remittances are an essential anti-poverty tool, comprising a significant share of national economic activity. Tajikistan, for example, has been dependent on remittances since an armed conflict between 1992 and 1998 claimed over 100,000 lives, destroying the economic infrastructure.[15] Approaching 20 years after the end of the conflict, remittances account for around 47% of national GDP.

In nine countries, the total value of remittances exceeds 20% of their total GDP. There are 12 countries on both lists, having large total volumes of remittances that also comprise a substantial share of GDP: Bangladesh, the Dominican Republic, El Salvador, Guatemala, Honduras, Jordan, Lebanon, Pakistan, the Philippines, Nepal, Serbia, Sri Lanka and Tajikistan.

The United States is the largest destination for international migrants and by far the largest source of global remittances. The World Bank records $56.3 billion in official remittance outflows from the United States in 2014. After the United States, the next largest sources of remittances in 2014 were:; Saudi Arabia ($36.9 billion); Russia ($32.6 billion); Switzerland ($24.7 billion) and Germany ($20.8 billion) and other advanced European economies.[16]

The IMF, World Bank, and the U.S. government do not compile and publish remittance flows from the United States (or other countries) to individual countries or regions. However, since 2010, the World Bank has estimated bilateral remittance flows between its member countries.[17] **Table 2** presents the World Bank's estimates for the largest recipients of remittances from the United States.

Table 2. Estimated Remittances from the United States, 2010-2015 (Billions of U.S. Dollars)

	2010	2011	2012	2013	2014	2015
Mexico	21.69	23.17	22.81	22.59	24.00	24.32
China	11.40	13.31	13.07	15.15	15.85	16.25
India	9.37	10.86	11.96	11.11	11.19	10.96
Philippines	9.33	10.00	10.60	9.08	9.65	9.68
Vietnam	4.70	4.88	5.68	6.22	6.81	7.45
Guatemala	3.78	4.03	4.40	4.87	5.28	5.98
Nigeria	5.92	6.14	6.13	5.73	5.74	5.67
El Salvador	3.09	3.29	3.56	3.63	3.87	3.99
Dominican Republic	2.71	2.87	2.73	3.34	3.58	3.83
Honduras	2.30	2.50	2.58	2.74	2.94	3.26

Source: World Bank, Bilateral Remittances Matrices, various years.

THE U.S. REMITTANCE MARKETPLACE

Money Service Businesses (MSBs)

Currently, the U.S. foreign remittance market is dominated by MSBs, a category of non-bank financial institutions that generally own proprietary, so-called "closed-loop" payment systems and operate largely outside of conventional banks.[18] The capacities of MSBs include money orders, traveler's checks, money transmission, check cashing, currency exchange, currency dealing, and stored value.[19] MSBs cover a broad variety of enterprises ranging from the small and simple to large firms with numerous branches or outlets. MSBs include the U.S. Postal Service, because it issues money orders. Western Union and MoneyGram are the two largest money transmitter companies and their agents are often located in a wide variety of other businesses, including supermarkets, check cashing agents, gas stations, liquor stores, convenience stores, and currency exchange offices. The main reason foreign remittance customers use MSBs is that they are often "unbanked;" that is, they do not have an account with a depository financial institution. In addition, money transmission services may be an ancillary service: the foreign remittance customer may be able to cash a paycheck, send money to family in his home country, and shop for groceries at the same location.

Traditional Financial Institutions

Remittance transactions are not a service traditionally provided by banks. International money transfer services provided by banks are expensive, and have thus been marketed primarily to corporate clients who send larger amounts than a typical migrant remitter. According to the Federal Reserve, the median amount of a consumer-initiated wire transfer processed by financial institutions is about $6,500 in domestic and foreign transfers, much larger than most remittance transactions, which are typically a few hundred dollars.[20] Another constraint for bank-provision of remittances is underdeveloped financial systems in many of the largest remittance-receiving countries. Since many recipients lack a bank account, they prefer to collect remittances money in cash. International wire transfer, however, is only an option when both the sender and receiver have access to deposit accounts at depository institutions. Unlike the "closed loop" payment system used by MSBs, banks and credit unions generally use "open loop" payment systems such as wire transfer systems and correspondent banking channels. MSBs, by acting through retail store locations such as grocery stores, often have more extensive distribution networks in the countries in which they operate than do traditional financial institutions.

As consumer demand for remittances has grown over the past two decades, banks and credit unions have shown a greater interest in directly providing remittances services to consumers. Remittance services can be a way to bring low-income migrants into the financial mainstream and introduce them to other financial products and services, such as interest-bearing savings accounts, checking accounts for paying bills (a replacement for money orders), free and secure check cashing services, and small dollar loans, among other services. Credit union participation has also been encouraged by the development of the World Council of Credit Unions' International Remittance Network, a credit union network for international money transfers.

To generate more remittances business, since 1998, U.S. depository institutions have had the option of transmitting remittance transfers through the Automated Clearing House (ACH) system. The ACH system is a system that clears and settles batched electronic transfers for participating depository institutions. Since financial transfers are batched together and sent on a fixed schedule, banks can charge a lower price than for traditional international wire transfers, which are sent individually. The originating institution combines the payment instructions from its various customers and sends them in a batch to an ACH operator—the U.S. Federal Reserve Banks' FedGlobal Payments Service or the Clearing House's Electronic Payments Network for processing. In addition to remittances, international ACH transfers are used for a range of small, recurring, cross-border payments such as social security and other benefit payments, business transactions such as vendor payments, and consumer transactions such as bill payments and remittance transfers.

Since 2001, the U.S. Federal Reserve has provided so-called "account-to-receiver" FedGlobal services that allow funds from accounts at a U.S. depository financial institution to be sent to unbanked receivers for retrieval at either a bank location or at a trusted, third-party provider. As of 2013, FedGlobal services are available to Europe, Mexico, Panama, and Latin America, covering 35 countries in total.[21]

Participation in the remittance market by banks and credit unions, while growing, is still limited. The U.S. Federal Reserve does not collect precise statistics on remittance transfers, but reports that in 2014, the two U.S. ACH operators handled 18.3 billion ACH transactions, of which 54.6 million (or 0.3%) were initiated by a business or a consumer, but not by the U.S. government.[22]

Mobile and other Emerging Payment Systems

In addition to remittance services provided by MSBs and traditional financial institutions, there has been a proliferation of new companies utilizing new technologies to provide remittances in recent years. Options include computer and mobile-based payments,[23] pre-paid cards, which can be cashed out at an ATM or spent at retail stores,[24] directed transfer options where the sender transmits funds directly to payments on behalf of the recipient,[25] and money transfers through social media.[26] A study conducted in July 2013 by the World Bank's Consultative Group to Assist the Poor (CGAP) found that there are 41 so-called "branchless" remittance providers in 2013, up from 10 in 2010.[27] CGAP also found that traditional remittance providers are introducing flat fees and transparent foreign exchange rates in response to the increased competition.

REGULATION OF REMITTANCE PROVIDERS

At the international level, international standards and principles governing remittances have been set by the Financial Action Task Force (FATF) and the Bank for International Settlements (BIS). In the United States, the operations of U.S. banks and credit unions are closely regulated and supervised at both the state and federal level. Foreign bank branches and agencies are also governed by a combination of state and federal statutes, provisions of which include licensing requirements and permissible activities. The primary focus of federal regulation is on anti-money laundering (AML) and combating the financing of terrorism (CFT). Individual state regulators, on the other hand, regulate the operations of federally-chartered banks and MSBs. Since October 2013, the U.S. Consumer Financial Protection Bureau (CFPB) has enforced various consumer protection measures included by Congress in the *Dodd-Frank Wall Street Consumer Protection Act* (Dodd-Frank).

International Standards and Principles

Global standards on remittances emerged over the past decade, largely due to concerns raised about unregulated money transfer services and their use in planning the September 11, 2001 terrorist attacks. International efforts have been negotiated at the FATF, an inter-governmental body comprising 34 countries and two regional organizations, including the United States, that develops and promotes policies and standards to combat money laundering and terrorist financing.[28] FATF was established in 1989 by the G-7 countries to implement the Vienna Convention Against Illicit Traffic in Narcotic Drugs and Psychotropic Substances, the first international agreement to criminalize money laundering. It is housed at the Organization for Economic Cooperation and Development (OECD) in Paris.

The FATF sets minimum standards and makes recommendations for its member countries. Each country must implement the recommendations according to its particular laws and constitutional frameworks. In 2001, FATF issued nine special recommendations to counter terrorist financing. For example, FATF Special Recommendation VI required FATF member countries to regulate all MSBs. In 2012, FATF revised its recommendations and Special Recommendation VI became FATF Recommendation 14 on Money or Value Transfer Services.[29] Several other recommendations are relevant for remittance providers, including recommendation 10 on wire transfers, recommendation 11 on record keeping, recommendation 16 on wire transfers, recommendation 18 on internal controls and foreign branches and subsidiaries, and recommendation 20 on suspicious transaction reporting.[30]

International efforts have also focused on improving the operational aspects of remittance transfers. In 2007, the BIS and the World Bank jointly issued *General Principles for International Remittance Services*, to "help to achieve the public policy objectives of having safe and efficient international remittance services, which require the markets for the services to be contestable, transparent, accessible and sound."[31] General Principle 3 states that "Remittance services should be supported by a sound, predictable, nondiscriminatory and proportionate legal and regulatory framework in relevant jurisdictions," and affirms the FATF recommendations, advocating that remittance providers comply with all relevant FATF recommendations. FATF maintains a mutual evaluation system and also provides oversight of non-member countries' AML/CFT regimes.

U.S. Anti-Money Laundering/Combating the Financing of Terrorism (AML/CFT) Efforts

In the United States, remittance providers, both banks and MSBs, are required to identify, assess and take steps to design and implement controls in compliance with their obligations under the U.S. Bank Secrecy Act (BSA). The BSA has been amended a number of times, most notably by Title III of the USA PATRIOT Act in 2001.[32] Among other things, Title III expanded the BSA framework beyond AML to also fight terrorist financing. The main purpose of the BSA is to require financial institutions to maintain appropriate records and file reports that can be used in criminal, tax, or regulatory investigations or proceedings. The Treasury Department's Financial Crimes Enforcement Network (FinCEN) administers the BSA on behalf of Treasury. With limited exceptions, MSBs are subject to the full range of BSA regulatory controls.

Remittance providers must conduct customer identification procedures for certain transactions, and maintain financial records. All MSBs must obtain and verify customer identity as well as record beneficiary information for funds transfers of more than $3,000. They must file Currency Transaction Reports (CTRs), for customer transactions of $10,000 or more in a day, and Suspicious Activities Reports (SARs) for dubious transactions of generally more than $2,000, that the remittance provider "knows, suspects, or has reason to suspect involves funds from illegal activity or is designed to conceal their origin, is designed to evade BSA obligations, or has no apparent business or law purpose."[33]

Remittances to certain foreign countries may also be subject to sanctions under various federal statutes administered by the Treasury Department's Office of Foreign Assets Control (OFAC). The U.S. Government only restricts remittances on countries, individuals, or companies that are subject to U.S. sanctions and embargoes. Furthermore, the Treasury Department does not have the authority to direct any financial institution to open or maintain a particular account or relationship. The decision to maintain any financial relationship is made by each financial institution itself, while complying with U.S. laws.

Given the relatively small percentage of financial crimes associated with terrorist financing (at this point in time), some analysts argue that regulations are excessively burdensome on the remittance providers, leading many to stop providing services completely. This is of greatest concern for customers sending money to low-income and post-conflict countries, many of which lack a formal financial sector.34 For example, Minnesota is home to the largest Somali-American population in the United States. Somalis in the United States send an estimated $100 million in remittances every year to Somalia. Over the past several years, U.S. and international financial institutions have refused to process payments to Somalia, in fear that they could not certify, to the government's satisfaction, whether funds transferred by them might eventually end up in the hands of terrorists, specifically the al-Qaeda affiliate Al-Shabaab. In December 2011, Minnesota- based Sunrise Community Banks, the last remaining financial institution willing to provide banking services to Somali-owned money brokers stopped providing banking services.

Consumer Protection

State-Licensing of Remittance Providers

Regulatory efforts at the state level are focused primarily on consumer protection. Most states have laws requiring money transmitters to be licensed by the state banking agency. Some of these states (usually those with significant immigrant populations) have specific licensing requirements for transmitters sending money to foreign countries. Of the 50 states, only Montana, New Mexico, and South Carolina do not require state licenses for MSBs.[35]

"Dodd-Frank" Measures

In response to concerns from U.S. immigrant communities raised during the 110th and 111th Congresses over inadequate disclosure of remittance fees and insufficient consumer protection for remittance transactions, Congress created new consumer protections as part of the *Dodd Frank Wall Street Reform and Consumer Protection Act (Dodd Frank).*[36] The Consumer Financial Protection Bureau (CFPB) released on April 30, 2013, a final rule implementing the Dodd-Frank remittance provisions. The effective date of the Final Rule is October 28, 2013.

Under the new law (Section 1073 of Dodd-Frank), a remittance transfer provider must provide consistent, reliable disclosure of the price of a transfer, the amount of currency to be delivered to the recipient, and the date of availability prior to the consumer making any payment. The new requirements also increase consumer protections by requiring remittance providers to investigate disputes and remedy errors related to the transaction.

During the rulemaking process, remittance providers raised concerns about the feasibility of disclosing third-party fees and taxes, which are often unknown prior to the transaction taking place, and the "error-resolution" provisions, given remittance providers' risk of loss and fraud due to remittance customers' providing incorrect information. To address industry concerns, the CFPB's Final Rule provides greater flexibility for remittance providers on the disclosure of third-party fees and taxes and exempts remittance providers from error remedy procedures due to errors made by the remittance customer, such as providing an incorrect account number for the recipient.[37]

While the new protections may decrease the cost of remittances over the long-run by improving transparency and potentially increasing competition, short-run cost increases may be significant. The increased cost to remittance providers for maintaining up-to-date information on exchange and tax rates of receiving countries and fees charged by third parties may likely be passed on to their customers. The error remedy requirement may also expose remittance transfer providers to potential litigation from fraudulent transactions.[38] At the same time, costs for remittance transactions may increase since bank fee income is capped elsewhere.[39]

REMITTANCES AND U.S. DEVELOPMENT POLICY

Various U.S. efforts in the past have attempted to harness remittances to promote foreign economic development by channeling remittances toward investment and by using remittances to bring a larger percentage of the remitting population into the formal financial sector.

Promoting Economic Development

For those in the developing and least developed countries, monthly remittances of just a few hundred dollars are enough to lift many out of poverty. For example, a 2011 study by the United Nations Conference on Trade and Development (UNCTAD), looking at 77 countries between 1970 and 2008, found that, on average, a 10% increase in remittances significantly reduces poverty in recipient countries.[40]

Despite many studies, it remains unclear whether remittances directly impact economic growth. There is, however, substantial evidence of the use of remittances to provide for food, shelter, and the provision of other goods. Given their role as an anti-poverty measure, most remittances are spent on consumable goods. An influential 2004 study by the Inter-American Development Bank found that in Mexico, for example, 78% of remittances were spent on household goods, 8% on savings, 7% on education, and 6% on the purchase of luxury goods, real estate, or for investment purposes.[41]

In 2011, the United States Agency for International Development (USAID) launched a public-private initiative called the Diaspora Networks Alliance, and intends to take a "leadership role in the development community by innovating and fostering partnership models to deepen and scale diasporas' engagement in home country development."[42] In September of 2010, then-Secretary of State Hillary Clinton announced a U.S. program partnering with

El Salvador and Honduras called the Building Remittance Investment for Development Growth and Entrepreneurship (BRIDGE) Initiative. Under the BRIDGE Initiative, strong in-country financial institutions in Honduras and El Salvador can partner with the United States and multilateral partners to help explore options, such as securitizing remittance flows, to use their remittance flows safely and soundly as an asset to raise lower-cost and longer-term financing for infrastructure, public works, and commercial development initiatives. USAID-supported market assessments confirmed the feasibility of BRIDGE's goals in Honduras and El Salvador; however, barriers to securitizing remittance flows remain significant. These include underdeveloped financial sectors in many remittance receiving countries and the relatively small size of developing country securitized debt.

Increased Access to Financial Services

Remittances can also promote "financial inclusion" – improving access and use of financial services in both the host and home countries. Between 50% and 100% of banks in developing countries provide remittance services, yet the number of remittance recipients in developing countries with access to other financial services (such as checking accounts or credit) remains low. At the same time, remittances can increase financial development by paving the way for recipients to demand and gain access to financial services.

The U.S. government has supported, in Mexico, a remittance service that allows U.S. financial institutions to pre-open an account for a third-party beneficiary in Mexico at one of over 2,100 banks, micro finance institutions, and credit unions. A 2011 study found that receiving remittances increases the likelihood of having an account by at least 11%. In the United States, as a larger number of banks provide remittance services, remittance senders are also becoming more familiar with traditional financial services and products, fostering the use of deposit accounts, insurance, and facilitating access to credit.

Regarding U.S. remittance customers' access to financial services and remittance, given the focus on capturing all remittance transactions in the formal financial sector, U.S. law creates no citizenship requirements for opening a bank account or using a remittance service. U.S. financial institutions and MSBs can accept foreign government issued identification cards, such as Mexico's *Matricula Consular* or Guatemala's *Tarjeta de*

Identification Consular, as customer identification if they meet certain minimum information requirements.

ISSUES FOR CONGRESS

Key issues on remittances that Members of Congress may want to consider include the following:

Regulation of Remittances

Members may wish to explore the current federal and state regulatory regime for remittance providers and customers. Effective and proportional regulation of remittances reduces corruption, enhances transparency, and facilitates a more robust business environment. Other observers, however, raise concerns about the costs for remittance providers (and subsequently consumers) of navigating the patchwork of banking and anti-money laundering regulation.[43] According to the Federal Reserve:

> [R]eports suggest that large depository institutions may be reducing or restricting correspondent banking relationships, which in turn may limit the ability of smaller depository institutions to provide remittance transfer services. Reports also suggest that depository institutions may be terminating the accounts of some nonbank payment providers that offer financial services to consumers, such as money services businesses. Without accounts at depository institutions, some nonbank payment providers may be unable to access the financial system and therefore may be unable to continue providing services, including remittance transfer services.[44]

Regarding licensing and supervision of remittance providers, recent reform proposals include assigning a single national regulator with responsibility for regulating the entire money transmission business or at a minimum, increasing coordination and harmonization of state and federal rules on MSBs.[45] There have been recent congressional efforts in this direction. For example, Representative Spencer Bachus introduced legislation in the 111th Congress, H.R. 4331, *The Money Services Business Compliance Facilitation Act of 2009*, that would have established an office of MSB compliance in the

U.S. Department of the Treasury, charged with ensuring that state and federal regulators coordinate standards for MSB licensing and registration.

Other legislation has been introduced, and passed, that aims to facilitate remittances services by making it easier for MSBs to comply with federal and state regulations. The *Money Remittances Improvement Act of 2014* (P.L. 113-156), signed into law on August 8, 2014, allows federal regulators, including FinCEN and the IRS, to rely on examinations conducted by state financial supervisory agencies if: (1) the category is required to comply with federal requirements, or (2) the state supervisory agency examines the category for compliance with federal requirements. According to Treasury, this legislation "should allow for better allocation of state and federal resources, better targeting of higher risk MSBs, and improved AML/CFT compliance across the [financial] industry."[46]

Others propose that U.S. policymakers should prioritize access to remittance services for highly impacted communities such as Somali-Americans. This may mean more money for technical assistance to boost the capacity of poorly regulated jurisdictions, such as Somalia. For example, the U.S. Treasury Department could help integrate Somali-American MSBs into an ACH payment system; help improve training of MSBs to improve monitoring of their agents; and/or help Somalia regulate its payment systems.[47]

Members of Congress may also explore the impact of the current regulatory regime on the development of emerging payments systems for sending remittances, such as mobile, card, or Internet-based models. Some observers argue that current federal and state money transmission laws may be inappropriate for new and emerging payments systems.[48] Remittance payments already touch many multiple regulatory agencies, and as mobile remittances services increase, the Federal Communications Commission (FCC) and the Federal Trade Commission (FTC) will likely play an increasing role. Mobile carriers and other alternative providers are less familiar than MSBs with U.S. and international banking laws and, the lack of U.S. guidance or framework for mobile payments creates coverage, liability, and AML/CFT concerns that Congress may move to explore.[49]

Members may also pay special attention to the implementation of the "Dodd-Frank" consumer protections following their October 2013 implementation. On one hand, some argue that the new protections will drive down the cost of remitting by requiring greater transparency of fees associating with money transfers. Others argue that the costs of new systems and increased liability for transaction problems will raise costs and deter MSBs and financial institutions from providing remittance services.[50]

Promoting Remittances as a Development Tool

Members of Congress may consider whether the U.S. government efforts on remittances should extend to influencing how they are spent. There are multiple viewpoints on the extent the U.S. government should promote remittances as a development tool. Many U.S. development aid officials, for example, are interested in understanding the economic impact of remittances on sending and receiving communities and developing policies to help channel remittances to their most productive use. Others argue that the remittances are foremost an anti-poverty tool, and that policymakers should be cautious about placing too much emphasis on remittances as a development tool or possibly confusing remittances with foreign aid. Importantly, remittances are a private transaction, and thus any official policy efforts, they argue, should be narrowly focused on reducing the cost of remittance transactions and creating additional opportunities for labor migration.[51]

Remittances and U.S. Immigration Policy

Members may consider the interplay of U.S. remittance policy efforts and U.S. immigration policy. Some Members of Congress, however, have raised concerns that current customer identification policies, which do not require a remittance customer to provide documentation of legal U.S. immigration status, may undermine efforts to enforce U.S. immigration laws. In light of this concern, Senator David Vitter has introduced S. 79, *Remittance Status Verification Act of 2015*, that would require remittance providers to impose a 7% fine on any sender of remittances that is unable to provide documentation of their legal status under U.S. immigration laws. Other efforts to restrict the ability of migrants to send remittances have been passed at the state-level.[52]

Some analysts argue, however, that restricting remittances through taxes or additional customer identification rules would not deter migration to the United States and would only drive remittances underground to informal methods of money transfer.[53] In addition to increased AML/CFT risk related to informal money transfer systems, shifting remittance flows to informal channels may impede policy efforts to use remittances as a means to promote access to financial services.

End Notes

[1] World Bank, Migration and Remittances Factbook 2016, December 2015.

[2] CRS Report R42988, *U.S. Immigration Policy: Chart Book of Key Trends*, by William A. Kandel and Ruth Ellen Wasem.

[3] Ibid.

[4] World Bank Remittances Database

[5] Orozco, Manuel, "Transnational Engagement, Remittances and Their Relationship to Development in Latin America and the Caribbean," *Institute for the Study of International Migration, Georgetown University*, July 1, 2005.

[6] Dilip Ratha, Supriyo De, Sonia Plaza, Kirsten Schuettler, William Shaw, Hanspeter Wyss, Soonhwa Yi , "Migration and Remittances – Recent Developments and Outlook" Migration and Development Brief, World Bank, April 26, 2016.

[7] Foreign Direct Investment (FDI) can be defined as cross-border investment by a resident entity in one economy with the objective of obtaining a lasting interest in an enterprise resident in another economy.

[8] The most recent official data on remittances and other resources are available at http://www.worldbank.org/migration.

[9] The IMF's Balance of Payments Yearbook includes annual aggregate and detailed time series for balance of payments and international investment position for countries.

[10] *International Transactions in Remittances: Guide for Compilers and Users.* Washington, DC: International Monetary Fund, 2009.

[11] Often regionally-based, alternative remittance systems, date back hundreds of years and were originally used to finance trade in regions where traveling with gold or other forms of payment was not safe. These systems go by various names including *Hue* (Vietnam), *Fei-Ch'ien* (China) *Phei Kwan* (Thailand) *Hundi* (South Asia), or *Hui Kuan* (Hong Kong).

[12] Remittances Prices Worldwide Issue n. 17, March 2016.

[13] Ibid.

[14] Freund, Caroline and Spatafora, Nikola, "Remittances: Transaction Costs, Determinants and Informal Flows," World Bank Policy Research Working Paper 3704, 2005.

[15] CRS In Focus IF10290, *Tajikistan*, by Christopher T. Mann, Gabriel M. Nelson, and Bolko J. Skorupski.

[16] World Bank Remittances Database, April 2016.

[17] The World Bank's bilateral remittances matrices are available at: http://www.worldbank.org/en/topic/migrationremittancesdiasporaissues/brief/migration-remittances-data. The World Bank uses two datasets to construct the Bilateral Remittance Matrix. The first is UN Population Division estimates of migrant stock by country of origin and destination, also used by this tool. The second dataset is remittance inflows data, constructed as the sum of three components in the IMF's Balance of Payments Statistics: (i) compensation of employees, (ii) workers' remittances, and (iii) migrants' transfers. A country's total remittance inflows in a given year are allocated to its emigrant stocks, adjusting for the migrant sending and receiving countries' per capita income.

[18] For example, a remittance-sender goes to a Western Union agent in Chicago to send money to her uncle in Brazil, who collects the funds from one of the more that 10,000 Western Union agents in Brazil. Since there are Western Union agents on both ends of the transaction, the transaction occurs outside the conventional banking system.

[19] Stored value is funds or monetary value represented in digital electronic format and stored or capable of storage on electronic media in such a way as to be retrievable and transferable electronically, such as a prepaid Visa gift card.

[20] Board of Governors of the Federal Reserve System, *Report to the Congress on the Use of the ACH System and Other Payment Mechanisms for Remittance Transfers to Foreign Countries,* May 2015.

[21] The European service includes Austria, Belgium, Cyprus, Czech Republic, Denmark, Finland, France, Germany, Greece, Ireland, Italy, Luxembourg, Malta, Netherlands, Poland, Portugal, Slovakia, Slovenia, Spain, Sweden, Switzerland, and United Kingdom. The Latin American service includes Argentina, Brazil, Columbia, Costa Rica, El Salvador, Guatemala, Honduras, Mexico, Nicaragua, Peru, and Uruguay. The Latin American service, which only involves account-to-receiver ACH transfers, is in addition to the account-to-account service for Mexico.

[22] Board of Governors of the Federal Reserve System, *Report to the Congress on the Use of the ACH System and Other Payment Mechanisms for Remittance Transfers to Foreign Countries,* April 2013.

[23] Examples include Xoom (Global), Globe GCASH (Philippines) and Safaricom M-PESA (Kenya and Tanzania).

[24] Examples include iRemit Visa (Asia) and mPower Yap Card (Global).

[25] Examples include Regalo Pay (Central and South America) and WillStream (Africa).

[26] Examples include Azimo and Fastacash, which allow transfer between Facebook users.

[27] World Bank Consultative Group on the Poor (CGAP), *CGAP Landscape Study on International Remittances through Branchless Banking*, February 2012.

[28] Members of FATF are Argentina, Australia, Austria, Belgium, Brazil, Canada, China, Denmark, the European Commission, Finland, France, Germany, Greece, the Gulf Cooperation Council, Hong Kong, Iceland, India, Ireland, Italy, Japan, Korea, the Netherlands, Luxembourg, Mexico, New Zealand, Norway, Portugal, Russia, Singapore, South Africa, Spain, Sweden, Switzerland, Turkey, the United Kingdom, and the United States. See CRS Report RS21904, *The Financial Action Task Force: An Overview*, by James K. Jackson.

[29] The Financial Action Task Force, *The FATF Recommendations: International Standards on Combating Money Laundering and the Financing of Terrorism and Proliferation*, February 2012.

[30] Ibid.

[31] Bank for International Settlements and the World Bank, *General Principles for International Remittance Services*, January 2007.

[32] CRS Report RL31208, *International Money Laundering Abatement and Anti-Terrorist Financing Act of 2001, Title III of P.L. 107-56 (USA PATRIOT Act)*, by M. Maureen Murphy.

[33] *Treasury/FinCEN Report to Congress in Accordance with Section 359 of the USA PATRIOT Act*, Department of the Treasury, November 2002.

[34] Natter, Raymond, "Dodd-Frank Act and Remittances to Post-Conflict Countries: The Law of Unintended Consequences Strikes Again," *Loyola Consumer Law Review*, Vol. 25, 2013.

[35] Taylor, Jennifer R. and Emre N. Ilter, "Domestic and Foreign Money Transmitters Face Complex Hazardous Web of Federal and State Laws and Regulations," *Financial Fraud Law Report*, February 2013.

[36] For example, see: *Remittances: Access, Transparency, and Market Efficiency: A Progress Report: Hearing before the House Committee on Financial Services, Subcommittee on Domestic and International Monetary Policy, Trade, and Technology*., 110th Congress, May 17, 2007; and *Remittances: Regulation and Disclosure in a New Economic Environment*, Hearing before the House Committee on Financial Services, Subcommittee on Financial Institutions and Consumer Credit, 111th Congress, June 3, 2009.

[37] Habib, Azba, "A Summary of the Final Remittance Transfer Rule (Section 1073)," *Retail Payments Risk Forum*, May 2013.

[38] World Bank, *Migration and Development Brief No. 19*, November 20, 2012.

[39] For example, see CRS Report R41913, *Regulation of Debit Interchange Fees*, by Darryl E. Getter and CRS Report R42744, *U.S. Implementation of the Basel Capital Regulatory Framework*, by Darryl E. Getter.

[40] According to the study, holding all else equal, a 10% increase in remittances was found to reduce the poverty gap by about 3–5% depending on how the poverty gap is measured ($1.25 a day or $2.00 a day). "Impact of Remittances on Poverty in Developing Countries," *United Nations Conference on Trade and Development*, 2011.

[41] Inter-American Development Bank, *Sending Money Home: Remittance to Latin America and the Caribbean*, May 2004.

[42] USAID, *Diaspora Networks Alliance: Framework for Leveraging Migrant Resources for Effective Development and Diplomacy*, 2012.

[43] Clay Lowery and Vijaya Ramachandran, *Unintended Consequences of Anti-Money Laundering Policies for Poor Countries*, Center for Global Development, Washington, DC, 2015.

[44] Board of Governors of the Federal Reserve System, *Report to the Congress on the Use of the ACH System and Other Payment Mechanisms for Remittance Transfers to Foreign Countries,* May 2015.

[45] Watterson, Collin, "More Flies with Honey: Encouraging Formal Channel to Combat Money Laundering," *Texas Law Review*, Vol. 91, 2013.

[46] Daniel L. Glaser, *Treasury's Work to Support Money Transmitters*, U.S. Department of the Treasury, Treasury Notes, Washington, DC, August 10, 2014.

[47] Orozco, Manuel and Julia Yansura, "Keeping the Lifeline Open: Remittances and Markets in Somalia," *Oxfam America, African Development Solutions, and the Inter-American Dialogue*, July 2013.

[48] Tu, Kevin, "Regulating the New Cashless World," *Alabama Law Review*, Vol. 65, Issue 1, 2013.

[49] Mark E. Budnitz, *The Legal Framework of Mobile Payments: Gaps, ambiguities, and overlap*, Pew Charitable Trust, Washington, DC, February 10, 2016.

[50] Witkowski, Rachel, "How CPFB's Remittance Rule Will Reshape Global Money Transfers," *American Banker*, May 20, 2013.

[51] Rosser, Ezra. "Immigrant Remittances," *Connecticut Law Review*, Vol. 41, No. 1, November 2008. See also, Feibelman, Adam, "The Very Uneasy Case Against Remittances: An Ex Ante Perspective," *North Carolina Law Review*, Vol. 88, 2010.

[52] In 2009, Oklahoma introduced a $5 tax on remittances plus an additional 1% charge on amounts of $500. The drafter of Oklahoma's remittance tax provision law justified it because the law "burdens mostly illegal immigrants and drug traffickers from Mexico who wire illegal proceeds back to their home country." Murphy, Sean. "Oklahoma Lawmaker Defends Wire Money Transfer Tax," *Salon.com*, April 12, 2010.

[53] Mohaptra, Sanket, "Taxing Remittances is not a good idea," *World Bank*, December 18, 2012.

In: International Remittances
Editor: Cameron Slaton
ISBN: 978-1-53610-158-4

Chapter 2

INTERNATIONAL REMITTANCES: ACTIONS NEEDED TO ADDRESS UNRELIABLE OFFICIAL U.S. ESTIMATE*

United States Government Accountability Office

WHY GAO DID THIS STUDY

For many countries, remittances represent a large and stable source of foreign currency. Remittances have received increasing attention from policymakers as the volume of funds transferred has increased over the years. Despite the global significance of remittances, much remains unknown about the actual volume of remittances and the methods used to remit them. GAO was asked to study the potential effects of a fine on certain remitters and estimates of U.S. remittances. GAO examined (1) the potential effects of a fine on remitters unable to provide proof of legal immigration status, and (2) BEA's remittance estimate and the extent to which its revised estimation methodology met government-wide policies and best practices. GAO constructed a hypothetical scenario analysis to show the uncertainty associated with the effects of a fine. GAO interviewed, among others, BEA, International Monetary Fund and World Bank officials, and researchers. GAO also analyzed BEA's estimate of U.S. remittances and documentation of its methodologies.

* This is an edited, reformatted and augmented version of a United States Government Accountability Office, Publication No. GAO-16-60, dated February 2016.

What GAO Recommends

GAO recommends that BEA conduct analyses to improve the reliability of its estimate and follow established policies for documenting its methods and analyses. BEA agreed to implement the recommendations but disagreed that its estimates are unreliable and not adequately documented. GAO disagrees and maintains that BEA's revised estimation model produces unreliable estimates and BEA could not provide adequate documentation of its methodology.

What GAO Found

The Remittance Status Verification Act of 2015, S. 79, would require remittance transfer providers to request that all senders of remittances to recipients outside the United States provide proof of their legal status under U.S. immigration laws and impose a fine on those unable to provide such proof. The funds collected would be submitted to the Consumer Financial Protection Bureau (CFPB) to pay for its administrative and enforcement costs in carrying out the act, and any remaining funds would be used to pay expenses related to border protection. The fine may raise money for border protection, but the exact amount is unknown and would depend on several factors, including

- the dollar amount of remittances sent by those without legal status,
- changes in remitter behavior due to the fine, such as using unregulated transfer methods, and
- CFPB's administrative and enforcement costs to carry out the act.

The first two factors above affect the volume of remittances that would be subject to a fine. The third factor affects the amount of net revenue from the fine remaining for border protection. Finally, remittance transfer providers told GAO that the fine could have consequences for them, including potentially disproportionate costs for small providers.

The Bureau of Economic Analysis (BEA) estimated that remittances from the United States were approximately $40 billion in 2014. However, BEA's methodology for estimating remittances is not consistent with government-wide policies and guidance on statistical practices or with BEA's own best practices and thus produces unreliable estimates. GAO identified several weaknesses in BEA's estimation methodology, illustrated by the following examples.

- BEA failed to use appropriate methodology that addressed questionable aspects of the data, such as missing information and measurement problems. This is inconsistent with National Research Council of the National Academies of Science guidelines for federal statistical agencies and government-wide policies.
- BEA also calibrated the output of the new model to match the estimate produced by BEA's previous model. BEA did this because according to officials the new model produced substantially lower results than BEA had previously estimated. In a 2006 report GAO had questioned the reliability of BEA's previous model; as a result BEA's actions raise further concerns about the reliability of the new model's results.

Moreover, BEA could not provide adequate, transparent documentation underlying its methodology or reviews of its methods and data. According to BEA officials, BEA did not adhere to its own best practices for changing its methodology because they did not consider the remittance estimate to be influential information. However, BEA's estimate is influential, as it is cited by national and international organizations and in some cases is incorporated into the estimates of these organizations, including the World Bank.

ABBREVIATIONS

ACS	American Community Survey
AML	anti-money laundering
BEA	Bureau of Economic Analysis
BSA	Bank Secrecy Act
Census Bureau	United States Census Bureau
CFPB	Consumer Financial Protection Bureau
Commerce	Department of Commerce
CPS	Current Population Survey
Dodd-Frank Act	Dodd-Frank Wall Street Reform and Consumer Protection Act
EFTA	Electronic Fund Transfer Act

FCSM	Federal Committee on Statistical Methodology
FinCEN	Financial Crimes Enforcement Network
IDB	Inter-American Development Bank
IARIW	International Association for Research in Income and Wealth
IMF	International Monetary Fund
IQA	Information Quality Act
MESC	Modernization and Enhancement Steering Committee
NRC	National Research Council
OECD	Organization for Economic Co-operation and Development
OMB	Office of Management and Budget
R2	R-squared
Treasury	Department of the Treasury

* * *

February 16, 2016

The Honorable David Vitter
United States Senate

The Honorable Tom Price
Chairman
Committee on the Budget
House of Representatives

The United States is the largest remittance sending country in the world with an estimated $54.2 billion sent in 2014, according to the World Bank.[1] For many receiving countries, remittances are the largest source of foreign currency, often amounting to more than official foreign assistance from international aid organizations and developed countries such as the United States. These transfers are generally considered a stable source of funds for receiving countries.

In a March 2006 report we examined various methods of estimating remittances from the United States and found that different methodologies had resulted in a range of estimates.[2] We reviewed the model that the Bureau of Economic Analysis (BEA) used to estimate U.S. remittance flows and found that the estimate was uncertain because of issues with the quality and timeliness of the data.

According to the International Monetary Fund (IMF), remittances have received increasing attention from policymakers in many nations and international organizations as the volume of funds transferred has grown over the years. However, despite their global and economic significance, much remains unknown about the actual volume of remitted funds and the methods used to remit them. Concerns about the reliability and consistency of remittance estimates from the Group of Eight and other international observers have led to the creation of a guide that aims to substantially improve the quality of remittance data.[3] In 2009, the Luxembourg Group on Remittances, which included representatives from the IMF, World Bank, Organization for Economic Co-operation and Development (OECD), Eurostat and national statistical offices and central banks from countries around the world, produced detailed guidance that includes recommendations for best practices in collecting information about and estimating remittances.[4]

In January 2015, the Remittance Status Verification Act of 2015 was introduced in the U.S. Senate.[5] The proposed legislation would amend the Electronic Fund Transfer Act (EFTA) to require remittance transfer providers to request that all senders of remittance transfers to recipients outside of the United States provide proof of their legal status under the immigration laws.[6] The proposed legislation would require remittance transfer providers to impose a fine on any sender unable to provide proof of immigration status and would also include a provision for GAO to study the act's effects. In states that require proof of legal residence, acceptable documentation for showing proof of legal status under the proposed law would include a state-issued driver's license or federal passport, or the same documentation as required by the state for proof of identity for the issuance of a driver's license or as required for a federal passport.[7] For those states that do not require proof of legal residence, under the proposed law the Consumer Financial Protection Bureau (CFPB) would define by rule what constitutes acceptable documentation of proof of legal status.

Each remittance transfer provider would be required to impose on any sender unable to provide proof of legal immigration status a fine equal to 7 percent of the dollar amount to be transferred, excluding any fees or other charges imposed by the remittance transfer provider. The provider would then be required to submit all fines imposed and collected to CFPB to pay for the administrative and enforcement costs to CFPB of carrying out the act. Any funds remaining after paying for such costs would be transferred by CFPB to the Department of the Treasury (Treasury) to be used to pay expenses relating to U.S. Customs and Border Protection for border security fencing, infrastructure, and technology. The bill was referred to the Committee on Banking, Housing, and Urban Affairs on January 7, 2015.

You asked that we consider the potential effect on remitters and providers of the proposed Remittance Status Verification Act and the potential revenue the proposed act would generate, and that we update our previous work on estimates of remittances from the United States. This report (1) discusses the potential effects of assessing a fine on remitters unable to provide proof of legal U.S. immigration status, and (2) examines BEA's remittance estimate and the extent to which its revised estimation methodology met government-wide policies and agency best practices.

To discuss the potential effects of assessing a fine on remitters unable to provide proof of U.S. immigration status, we summarized estimates of the number of immigrants without legal status from federal agencies and research organizations, including the Department of Homeland Security (DHS), Pew Research Center, and Center for Migration Studies (CMS). Collectively, DHS, Pew Research, and CMS are primary sources for the estimates of immigrants without legal status in the United States, according to researchers we interviewed. We used these sources to identify the size of the potentially affected group of immigrants without legal status. We also reviewed laws and regulations relevant to remittance transfer providers and interviewed providers. We spoke with regulators, including CFPB and the Financial Crimes Enforcement Network (FinCEN), and two industry associations to obtain their perspectives on compliance with the requirements of S. 79, should it become law.

In addition, we judgmentally selected a cross-section of remittance transfer providers that included five nondepository remittance transfer providers and four depository institutions based on a number of factors, including the volume of remittances and diversity of countries serviced. We interviewed academic researchers with expertise in remittances and immigration to the United States. Finally, we constructed a set of hypothetical scenarios using factors that would affect the amount of revenue generated for border protection. We varied the following factors to highlight the uncertainty associated with estimates of net revenue from the fine: dollar amounts of remittances sent by immigrants without legal status, the percentage reduction in remittances in response to the fine, and administrative and enforcement costs associated with the fine. Together, these three factors demonstrate the wide variation in potential net revenue from the fine. We found insufficient literature upon which to base the values given to each factor, therefore dollar amounts or percentages in our scenario analysis are hypothetical.

To describe BEA's estimate of remittances from the United States, we collected published estimates of personal transfers attributable to BEA. To examine BEA's current estimation methodology, we reviewed BEA documentation, including components of its model, and interviewed BEA officials. We obtained documentation on the Census Bureau's (Census) American Community Survey (ACS) and Current Population Survey (CPS) data to understand how they were used in BEA's remittance estimation methodology and interviewed Census officials familiar with the surveys. As described in this report, we found that results from BEA's estimation model are unreliable.

To obtain a variety of views about remittance estimation, including the challenges involved, we interviewed officials from Inter-American Development Bank (IDB), IMF, World Bank, and selected central banks from among the top 10 recipient countries of U.S. outflows that use a formal methodology to track remittance inflows or outflows on at least an annual basis, including Mexico and the Philippines.

We conducted this performance audit from October 2014 to February 2016 in accordance with generally accepted government auditing standards. Those standards require that we plan and perform the audit to obtain sufficient, appropriate evidence to provide a reasonable basis for our findings and conclusions based on our audit objectives. We believe that the evidence obtained provides a reasonable basis for our findings and conclusions based on our audit objectives.

BACKGROUND

The United States is home to more immigrants than any other country in the world.[8] Census estimated that 41 million foreign-born individuals resided in the United States from 2010 through 2014, making up 13 percent of the population.[9] According to the World Bank, the United States is also, by far, the largest source of remittances from foreign-born residents to their home countries, including Mexico, China, India, and the Philippines, among others (see fig. 1).

Remittance funds can be used for basic consumption, housing, education, and small business formation and can promote financial development in cash-based economies. In a number of developing economies, remittances have become an important and stable source of funds that exceeds revenues from exports of goods and services and financial inflows from foreign direct investment.

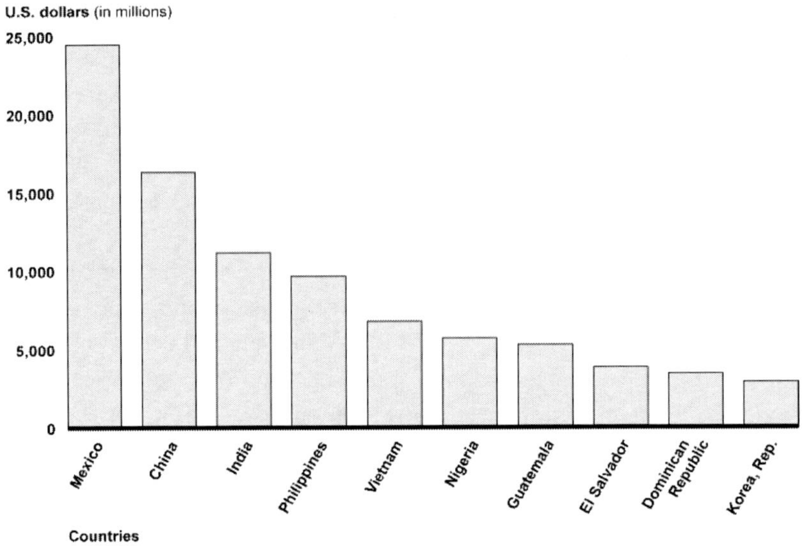

Source: GAO analysis of World Bank's Bi-lateral Remittance Matrix: United States outflows, 2014. | GAO-16-60.

Note: According to the World Bank, the remittance amounts in the bilateral remittance matrix are unofficial estimates designed to capture country-specific, disaggregated bilateral remittance estimates and have been published by the Migration and Remittances program office since 2010. In contrast to the World Bank's official remittance estimates, the World Bank's bilateral remittance estimates use a different methodology, and have higher remittance estimate totals per country. World Bank bilateral remittance data for 2014 are disaggregated using host country and origin country incomes and estimated migrant stocks from 2013.

Figure 1. Remittances Sent from the United States to Major Receiving Countries in 2014.

Remittances can be sent through formal transfer systems and informal methods. Formal systems typically include banks, credit unions, money transfer businesses such as wire services, and postal services. In the United States, providers of remittance transfer services (including bank and nonbank institutions) are subject to federal oversight and, depending on the state in which they operate, can be subject to supervision by states.[10] According to CFPB, nonbank remittance transfer providers sent an estimated 150 million individual transfers from the United States in 2012. Informal remittance transfer methods include hand-carried cash, courier services, and agents known as hawalas.[11]

Individuals can transfer remittance funds in several ways, such as

1. cash payments to individuals and bank accounts;
2. prepaid debit or credit cards; and
3. online and through mobile devices.

Global remittance estimates are published annually by some international organizations on an annual basis. IMF collects data on components of remittances submitted by its member countries, including the United States, as part of its annual publication of balance of payments statistics.[12] IMF's *Balance of Payments and International Investment Position Manual* provides a framework for identifying individual remittance flows that benefit households. According to IMF, this framework can be applied by all countries and should lead to some level of comparability among them. The World Bank uses IMF statistics to produce an annual Migration and Remittances Factbook and monthly and annual remittances data on its website.[13] Other international organizations, such as the IDB through the Multilateral Investment Fund, also produce annual reports on remittance estimates. In the United States, BEA is responsible for compiling the official U.S. estimates. Other nations may delegate the official estimation of remittances to central banks or specific government agencies.

In response to requests from policymakers, remittance data compilers, and other data users, IMF and the World Bank published a guide for compilers and users of remittances data.[14] The purpose of the guide is to promote lasting improvements in remittances data, which it seeks to accomplish by summarizing the definitions and concepts related to the balance of payments framework and by providing practical compilation guidance. Two items in the guide that substantially relate to remittances are "personal transfers" and "compensation of employees," both of which countries are required to report to IMF. Personal transfers are a measure of all transfers in cash or in kind made or received by resident households to or from nonresident individuals and households. Compensation of employees is a measure of the income of short-term workers in an economy where they are not resident and of the income of resident workers who are employed by a nonresident entity. The guide also defines additional measures related to remittances, which countries are encouraged but not required to report. For example, personal remittances represent the sum of personal transfers, net compensation of employees, and capital transfers between households, according to the guide.[15]

Institutions use different methodologies to produce estimates of remittances. For example, BEA uses demographic and household survey data and a model that calculates the remittance rates by demographic group to create the official estimate of remittances from the United States. The World Bank has developed its own methodology to create remittance estimates. Its research group produces country-specific development indicators and international development statistics. The World Bank then complements these data with information from the IMF's *Balance of Payments and International Investment Position Manual* to create annual and semi-annual remittance estimates.

Since 2010, researchers at the World Bank have also used United Nations population data to develop a bilateral migration matrix, which provides a second set of country-specific bilateral remittance estimates— that is, estimates between sending and receiving countries. These estimates are based on the number of migrants in different destination countries and estimates of how changes in the income of migrants influence the remittances they send. IDB's Multilateral Investment Fund has a different methodology, using estimates reported by central banks to IMF as a baseline for individual country estimates. The Multilateral Investment Fund then works with the Center for Latin American Monetary Studies to help refine remittance estimates for selected countries in the Latin America and Caribbean region.

Finally, some central banks use a combination of methods to estimate remittances. The central bank of Mexico, known as Banco de México, tracks remittance flows to Mexico with the help of regulatory reporting requirements on money transmitters. Since 2003, Mexico's methodology for estimating remittances has required firms that receive remittances to report, on a monthly basis, the amount of money received and the number of transactions conducted between the United States and Mexico. To track remittances through informal channels, such as couriers that fall outside this regulatory framework, Banco de México conducts a survey at the U.S.-Mexico border of Mexicans entering the country. The central bank of the Philippines, known as Bangko Sentral Ng Pilipinas, estimates remittances that are channeled through banks. The Philippine government also has established a formal program for registering and tracking overseas Filipino workers. This program provides data to the government on the type of employment these workers obtain as well as their salaries. The Bangko Sentral Ng Pilipinas also uses the *Survey of Overseas Filipinos* to supplement data from the program. Using these two approaches,

Bangko Sentral Ng Pilipinas is able to identify remittance funds sent by Filipinos overseas through friends and relatives and amounts brought in when these workers return home.

POTENTIAL EFFECT OF A FINE ON REMITTERS WITHOUT LEGAL STATUS IS UNCERTAIN AND DEPENDS ON A VARIETY OF FACTORS

A proposed fine on immigrants unable to show proof of legal status who send money through remittance transfer providers covered under EFTA could raise money for border protection, but the potential amount of revenue to be generated is unknown. Net revenue from the fine—the total of all fines collected less CFPB's administrative and enforcement costs— would depend on several key factors, namely the dollar amount of remittances sent by those without legal immigration status, changes in remitter behavior because of the fine, including a potential reduction in remittances through regulated providers, and the cost of enforcement. For example, the ability to raise money depends on a significant number of individuals without legal status using regulated remittance transfer providers and paying the fine. However, a fine could result in a decrease in remittances in the regulated market and an increase in remittances through informal methods of money transfer. The revenue raised by the proposed fine would first be used to pay CFPB for enforcement costs. We did not identify any estimates of the administrative and enforcement costs associated with the fine. Our hypothetical scenario analysis illustrates the sensitivity of potential net revenue estimates to these factors. CFPB and other federal regulators would enforce the requirements of the proposed legislation and CFPB identified some implementation challenges. Lastly, providers told us the fine could have consequences for them, and one provider said that smaller providers would likely be affected the most.

Several Factors Could Affect the Amount of Revenue Generated from a Proposed Fine on Remitters without Legal Status, as Hypothetical Scenarios Show

A fine could potentially generate net revenue for border control, but the following selected factors would influence the actual amount:

- The dollar amount of remittances sent by those without legal immigration status. The revenue raised by the fine would depend on the dollar amount of remittances sent by those individuals in the United States without legal immigration status and, specifically by those using regulated remittance transfer providers. According to three studies we identified during discussions with experts, estimates of unauthorized U.S. immigrants in 2012 ranged from 11.1 million to 11.4 million people.[16] Of that number, only those who conduct transactions through providers that are subject to EFTA would actually pay a fine, should they continue to use such providers, and that number is unknown.
- The response to the fine by individuals in the United States without legal status, including a reduction in remittances through regulated providers. If individuals without legal status respond to the fine by making money transfers that may not be subject to EFTA requirements, by remitting less, or leveraging connections with immigrants with legal status, the amount of revenue raised by the fine would be lower. Representatives from almost all of the organizations we spoke with, including providers, researchers, federal agencies, and community groups, stated that remitters without legal status may be deterred by the fine and the additional scrutiny around their immigration status. The amount of revenue generated by the fine would also depend on the extent to which those without legal immigration status continue to use regulated systems after the fine is imposed instead of switching to informal methods, such as hawalas. Two articles identified in our literature search noted that those without legal status may use methods that allow them to maintain a higher degree of anonymity. For example, those without legal immigration status may have relatives or friends who are authorized to be in the United States send remittances for them, potentially lowering the amount of revenue raised by a fine.[17]

Conversely, if most remitters continue to remit the same amount, and continue to remit through regulated channels, the total amount remitted may remain stable, and more revenue will be raised. Research experts, officials from industry, community groups, and some federal agencies with which we spoke suggested that some remitters unable to provide proof of legal status may send the remittance and pay the fine, but the exact percentage is unknown. While the effect of the fine depends heavily on the remitting behavior of individuals without legal immigration status and their response to the fine, limited information exists on how many of these individuals remit or the extent to which they rely on regulated methods.[18] In the absence of definitive studies on remitting behavior, the extent to which immigrants use regulated or informal methods for remitting and how they will respond to price increases is unknown.[19]

If the costs of the fine, including costs for providers to implement the requirements of the proposed legislation, are passed on to the remitter in the form of a price increase, remitters might reduce the amounts or the frequency with which they remit. Information on price sensitivity—how senders respond to an increase in price—is limited. According to a CFPB report and a remittance transfer provider with whom we spoke, remitters' response to higher prices may partly depend on knowledge of other available options, including access to information about fees charged by other providers.[20] Behavioral changes could substantially limit the amount of revenue generated for border protection.

- Administrative and enforcement costs associated with the fine. Although the regulatory costs associated with the proposed legislation are unknown, CFPB officials told us that the agency would incur expenses associated with implementing the legislation and ensuring compliance. According to CFPB, these expenses would include the costs of developing rules, examining remittance transfer providers, and cooperating with other federal agencies on enforcement actions against noncompliant institutions. Other federal regulators also enforce EFTA for their regulated entities, and state regulators also may play a role in oversight of remittance transfer providers. As the revenue for the fine would be used first to reimburse CFPB for administrative and enforcement costs to carry out the proposed legislation, high costs to CFPB for these activities would mean less net revenue available for border protection.[21] Uncertainty in these costs would contribute to uncertainty in how much revenue remains for border protection.

Given the uncertainty related to these important factors, we constructed a scenario analysis to illustrate how the revenue generated for border protection could vary based on the values we assume for the following, given our starting assumptions about the total volume of remittances and proportion of those in the formal sector:

1. the dollar amount of remittances sent by immigrants without legal status,
2. the reduction in remittances through regulated providers in response to the request to show proof of legal status or pay a fine, and
3. the magnitude of administrative and enforcement costs to CFPB.

The scenarios are hypothetical because the factors used to generate the results were selected solely to demonstrate the uncertainty in how much revenue would be collected. They are not supported by empirical research or evidence. The selected scenarios we illustrate are from a larger number that we analyzed to examine how sensitive net revenue from fines is to the factors. The three factors shown in figure 2 illustrate the potentially wide variation in net revenue from fines. In our analysis, we begin by assuming that the total volume of remittances is $50 billion and 50 percent of the total volume of remittances is sent through regulated providers. The scenario analysis varies the three factors above, thereby demonstrating the breadth of uncertainty in potential net revenue.

As figure 2 demonstrates, when the factors vary potential net revenue from fines can change significantly. For example, one scenario with no change in the amount of remittances and low administrative and enforcement costs could provide $0.41 billion in potential net revenue for border protection. In contrast, another scenario with a 75 percent reduction in remittances after the fine and high administrative and enforcement costs would generate potential net revenue of only $0.01 billion. In some cases, the cost incurred by CFPB could be more than the revenue from the fine. For example, a small dollar amount of remittances sent by immigrants without legal status, large reductions in remittances, and high administrative and enforcement costs could lead to negative net revenue.[22] Obtaining reasonable estimates of net revenue would depend upon having accurate, reliable, and complete information on the amount immigrants without legal status remit and their response to a requirement for providers to request proof of legal status or assess a fine, as well as administrative and enforcement costs. In the absence of such information, the potential net revenue a fine would generate is unknown.

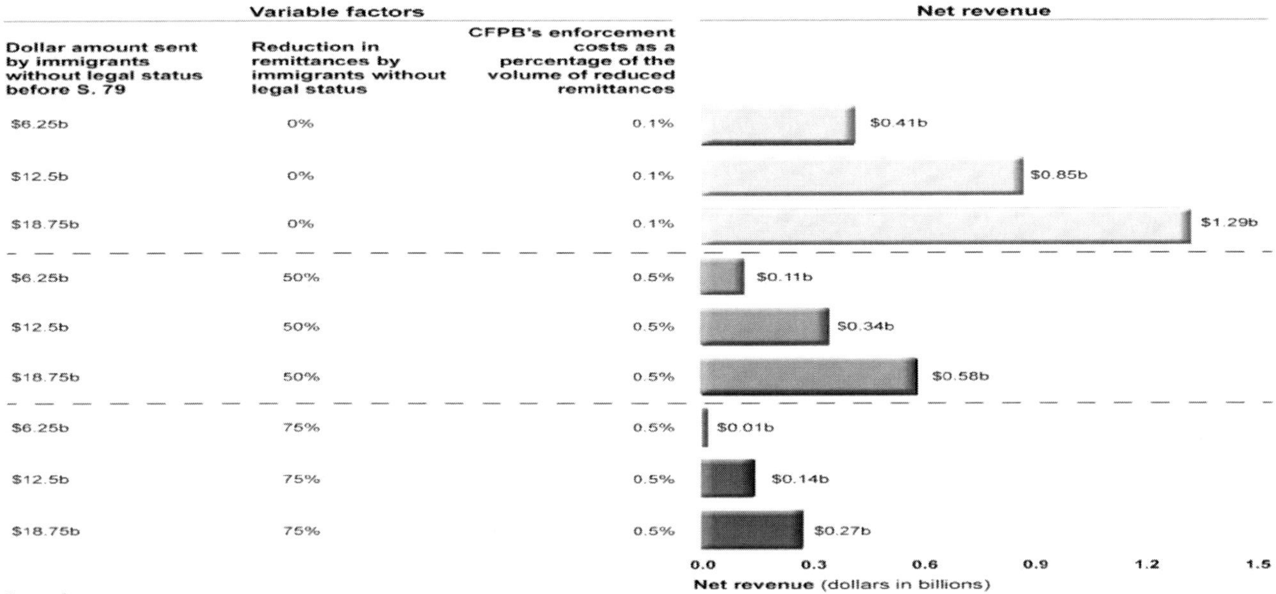

Legend

CFPB - Consumer Financial Protection Bureau

Source: GAO analysis. | GAO-16-60

Note: All amounts and percentages in figure 2 are hypothetical and demonstrate the uncertainty of the amount of potential net revenue from the fine. We assumed $50 billion in remittances and 50 percent of remittances in the regulated market. We made additional assumptions that we vary in the figure above:

a) $6.25 billion, $12.5 billion, and $18.75 billion in remittances are sent by individuals without legal status before the implementation of S. 79; b) after implementation, remittances might decrease such that the dollar amount of remittances is significantly smaller; and c) CFPB's costs are a percentage—0.1 percent or 0.5 percent—of the volume of remittances that remain in the regulated market after the reduction in remittances sent by immigrants without legal status. To calculate net revenue, we assumed dollar amount sent by immigrants without legal status before S. 79, less the percentage reduction in remittances, then multiplied by the 7 percent fine, less CFPB's administrative and enforcement costs. Varying these three assumptions demonstrates the variability in potential net revenue. Assumptions not included here would result in other amounts of potential net revenue.

Figure 2. Varying Selected Factors and Their Potential Effect on Revenue for Border Protection—A Hypothetical Scenario Analysis of the Proposed Legislation (S. 79).

Proposed Legislation Raises Other Issues for CFPB

Officials from CFPB noted that in addition to creating uncertainty about administrative and enforcement costs, the proposed legislation, if passed, would require CFPB to address other issues, including issuing new rules to define what constitutes proof of legal status and to establish procedures for submitting fines, as well as coordinating with other regulators.

- As noted earlier, CFPB would be required to define by rule what constitutes acceptable documentation in states that do not require proof of legal status to obtain a state-issued driver's license or a federal passport.
- CFPB would need to coordinate with other financial regulators. For example, the proposed legislation calls for remittance transfer providers to submit the fines to CFPB and for CFPB to then transfer to Treasury any remaining funds after the payment of CFPB's administrative and enforcement costs. However as noted previously, other federal regulators have the authority to enforce EFTA for the entities they supervise, including enforcing the remittance provisions against those supervised entities that are remittance transfer providers under the act. The proposed legislation would provide CFPB with rulemaking authority, but does not state how CFPB would coordinate with other agencies. CFPB staff told us that it might need to develop procedures with others on examination and enforcement efforts.[23]
- CFPB would be required to issue rules establishing the form and manner in which fines would be submitted to CFPB. CFPB staff told us that CFPB does not currently levy fines on consumers. Instead, CFPB levies monetary sanctions and brings other enforcement actions against consumer finance businesses and other persons in connection with violations of Federal consumer financial law. But CFPB staff noted that collecting fines directly from institutions for noncompliance is different from a fine on remitters collected by remittance transfer providers that is then submitted to the agency.
- Finally, CFPB may have examination authority over nonbank remittance transfer providers that also may be overseen by state regulators. If the proposed legislation were to become law, CFPB might have to coordinate with state regulators.

A Requirement for Proof of Legal Status or Payment of a Fine Would Also Affect Providers

If remittances decrease because the number of transactions or amounts remitted decline, the fee revenue associated with remittance transactions that providers receive would decrease. Without any corresponding reduction in cost, the decrease in remittances might decrease profits for some providers, but by how much is uncertain. Prior experience with legislation passed in Oklahoma in 2009 may demonstrate effects similar to those that could result from the proposed legislation though there are some key differences between the two.[24] The Oklahoma law imposed a $5 fee on each wire transfer from a nondepository institution, and 1 percent of the amount of the transaction, if any, in excess of $500.[25] When making a transfer, all persons regardless of immigration status were required to pay the fee. Under the Oklahoma law, customers who paid the fee are entitled to an income tax credit equal to the amount paid when filing individual income taxes in Oklahoma with either a valid Social Security number or a valid taxpayer identification number. The tax credit in effect means that those customers without a Social Security or taxpayer identification number are not eligible for the state income tax credit and therefore will have paid the remittance fee without being able to obtain a credit or refund.

Statements of four remittance transfer providers with operations in Oklahoma suggest that the law has had mixed effects. According to two providers, revenues decreased once the law was in place. Two providers told us that transaction activity in the state had fallen. One other provider stated that their company had still not recovered from the decline in revenue. This provider told us that the decreased number of transactions was the result of remittances that moved to out of state providers or from regulated to informal channels. The other two providers we interviewed noticed decreases in remittances, although they noted they did not have a large presence in Oklahoma. Also, one official from a state audit association noted that fee revenues for the State of Oklahoma continued to increase after the first year of the imposition of the fee.[26] Remittance transfer providers, industry associations, research experts, and some federal agencies we met with said that they expected to see revenues decrease in the regulated market if the proposed law (S.79) were passed, as it would send remittances to the informal market.

New proof-of-legal status requirements and fine collection could also increase remittance transfer providers' costs. Such potential costs were noted by almost all providers, and representatives from industry associations we spoke to. Several providers noted that they might need to pay for new computer infrastructure and databases, staff training, and compliance. One provider pointed out that just to add a new variable listing information on customers to an existing information system was a 9-month process that would involve testing and validation. Representatives of an industry association and one remittance transfer provider cited potential costs related to maintaining databases used to verify legal status.

Remittance transfer providers could also face increased compliance costs related to new requirements. In some cases, providers told us that compliance costs could be significant. For example, some providers said that they had made significant investments to comply with the fee and exchange rate disclosures and other requirements implemented through amendments to Regulation E after the passage of the Dodd-Frank Act, such as developing procedures to electronically disclose the fees charged by the provider. Another provider said that it had spent more than $3 million on technology enhancements and customer service teams to satisfy the requirements of the rule. Still another provider noted that the company spent about 3 percent to 4 percent of its revenue on the legal compliance budget.

One representative of a transfer provider whom we interviewed said that the company might be able to incorporate compliance requirements into its Bank Secrecy Act (BSA)/anti-money-laundering (AML) efforts. BSA/AML requirements for institutions that provide money transfer services include, among other things, collecting sender identification for each transfer in the amount of $3,000 or more.[27] Banks are also required to implement a customer identification program, under which they establish procedures specifying what identifying information they will collect when customers open accounts.[28] However, other providers noted that collecting identification is not the same as verifying legal status. For example, several providers accepted the Matrícula Consular de Alta Seguridad, which is an official identity card that Mexican Consulates issue to nationals living outside Mexico. As previously discussed, under the Remittance Status Verification Act this card would not be an acceptable form of identification for proving legal status within the United States for purposes of the act. One provider we spoke with explained that not all states require proof of legal status before issuing a driver's license or other form of identification. Forms of identification that demonstrate legal status may vary from state to state. It could be difficult for money transfer clerks to know what form of identification to collect, particularly when remitters may hold identification from other states.

Some providers and one trade association also noted that the proposed legislation would require additional staff training. For example, one provider said that the company operated through many retail outlets, such as grocery stores and gas stations, and it would not be practical to train all store clerks to determine the appropriate form of identification to show legal residency status. Another provider stated that it would be a significant challenge to train all agents—retail outlets that conduct transactions for the provider—on the documentation they would be responsible for collecting for proof of legal status. A trade association noted the difficulty and potential expense of training staff on how to properly check for proof of legal status; calculate, disclose, and collect the fine; and put the transaction in a database.

How much of the fine and added cost would be absorbed by the provider or retail outlet partly depends upon the competitiveness of the market. Remittance transfer providers stated that in competitive markets with a number of providers and a variety of methods for transmitting money, the demand for remittances is more sensitive to prices. For example, one provider indicated that it lost customers when its prices were only marginally higher than those charged by other providers. With the prospect of losing more customers and revenue, one provider with whom we spoke stated that it might choose to absorb some of the fine and added cost instead of passing it on. One provider we spoke with expected that the added costs would increase the costs passed on to consumers by 3 to 4 percentage points. If these costs were passed on in such a manner, all consumers, regardless of legal status, could experience an increase in the price of remittance transfers that are sent to a foreign country.

In addition, certain providers might be disproportionately affected by the requirements of the proposed legislation. According to representatives from two providers and a research expert, smaller providers generally operate at lower profit margins compared with larger providers.[29] Providers with lower margins would find it more difficult to absorb costs imposed due to the fine and may be more adversely affected with a reduction in revenues.

BEA Does Not Follow Best Practices for Estimating Remittances, Leading to an Unreliable Estimate

BEA's estimate of remittances from the United States totaled approximately $40 billion in 2014, and its estimates of remittances generally increased from 2006 to 2014. BEA changed its remittance estimation methodology in 2012 in order to incorporate new data on reported remittances. However, BEA's methodology for estimating remittances is not consistent with government-wide policies and guidance on statistical practices or with BEA's own best practices and thus produces unreliable estimates. For example, BEA did not follow the guidelines from the National Research Council (NRC) of the National Academies stating that data releases from a statistical program should be accompanied by appropriate methods for analysis that take account of variability and other sources of error in the data.[30] In addition, we identified several errors in BEA's analysis that led us to question the reliability of BEA's estimates, including data that are censored, measurement and coding errors, and an estimation methodology that is subject to biases.[31] Further, BEA calibrated its new model to match the estimates from BEA's old model, whose accuracy we questioned in a March 2006 report on remittance estimates. On the basis of discussions with BEA officials, BEA's failure to follow best practices appears to be due to the fact that the agency does not consider its remittance estimates to be "influential information" that is subject to a high degree of transparency. However, BEA's estimate is cited by national and international organizations and in some cases is incorporated into the estimates of these organizations, including the World Bank.

BEA's Estimates of Remittances from the United States

BEA's estimate of remittances from the United States (which it reports as personal transfers) totaled approximately $40 billion in 2014. As figure 3 shows, BEA's estimates of remittances generally increased from 2006 to 2014.

BEA's estimates of remittances from the United States are based on demographic and household survey data and a model that calculates the remittance rates by demographic group. BEA assumes that the foreign-born population represents the relevant population of remittance senders in the United States, because this population is most likely to have a personal link to foreign residents. The estimates of personal transfers include all current transfers from resident to nonresident households, regardless of the means of transfer.

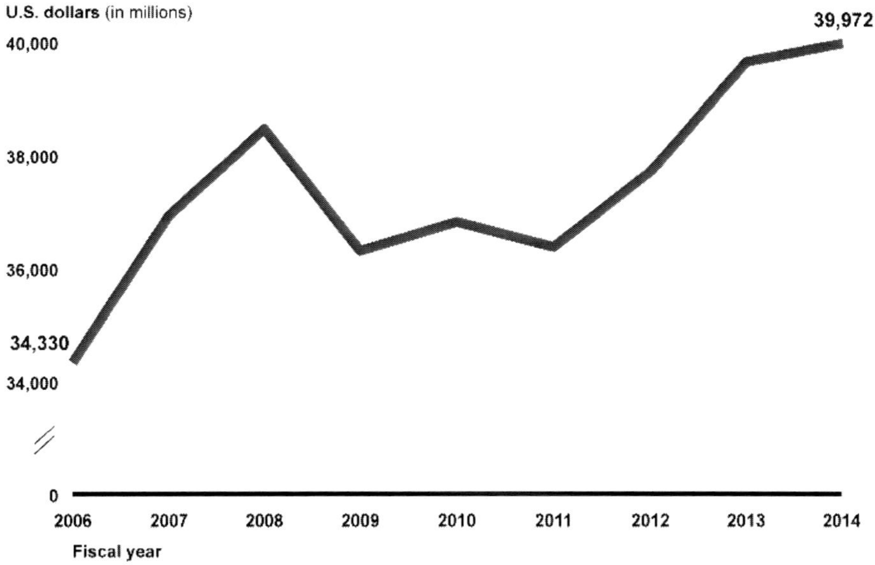

Source: GAO analysis of BEA Personal Transfer Data 2006-2014. | GAO-16-60.
Note: In GAO-16-60, we discuss the accuracy of BEA's personal transfer estimates.

Figure 3. Bureau of Economic Analysis' Estimate of Total Volume of United States Personal Transfers (Outflows) as Reported to the International Monetary Fund, 2006-2014.

BEA Changed Its Remittance Estimation Methodology in 2012 to Incorporate New Data on Reported Remittances

BEA changed its model for estimating remittances in 2012 by using new demographic variables and data on reported remittances from the August 2008 migration supplement to the Current Population Survey (CPS) conducted by Census.[32] For its revised model, BEA employed a multiplicative model—that is, a model whose results are the product of the combined effects produced by the individual variables. It used a nonstandard iterative technique to estimate the remittance rates.[33] These rates show the proportion of income that is remitted. To obtain total remittances, the remittance rates for different demographic categories can be multiplied by the number of individuals in those categories and their incomes. In its new methodology, BEA combined the new remittance rates from its revised model with ACS data on foreign-born residents and their income to estimate total remittances sent annually from the United States (see fig. 4).

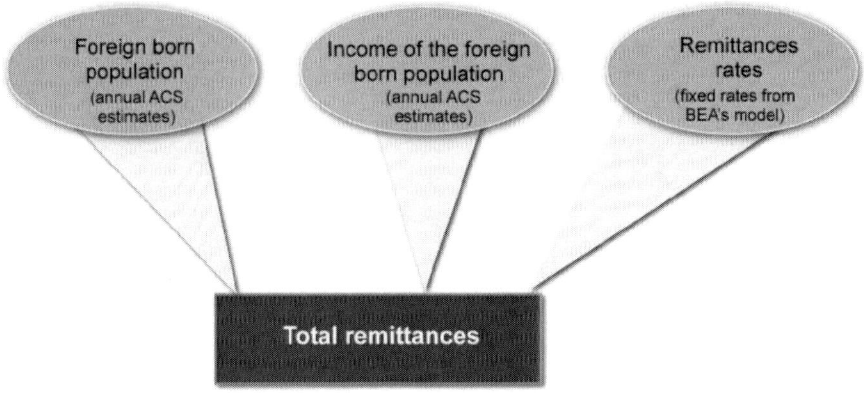

Legend
ACS – American Community Survey
BEA - Bureau of Economic Analysis
Source: GAO analysis. | GAO-16-60.

Figure 4. Basic Inputs to BEA's Current Remittance Estimation Model, as of 2012.

The availability of nationally representative data on remittances in the CPS with actual reported numbers on remittances provided BEA with an opportunity to revise the model it created in 2005.[34] BEA first tested its previous demographic variables against CPS data and found that its assumptions about family structure and time in the United States were weak indicators of how much people reported to remit in CPS data and that its previous country tiers did not match remitting behavior very well.[35] Therefore, in 2012 BEA changed the new model by,

- removing U.S. citizens born abroad of American parents, assuming that this group's remittance behavior would be similar to the behavior of U.S. born who were not included in their study;
- replacing the "children/no children" category with "married, spouse absent/other marital," because those in the latter category were more likely to send remittances to spouses abroad and were thus a better predictor of remittances;
- adding the category "living with roommates/other living arrangements," assuming that people shared housing to save money and therefore could send more remittances;
- combining immigrants who had been in the United States for 16 to 30 years with those who had been in the country for longer than 30 years

into one category, "15 plus years," as they found in CPS data that these two categories had similar remittance rates; and

- reallocating countries within pre-existing geographical tiers as BEA found that their previous country allocations were not the best match for the CPS data.[36]

BEA's Methodology Resulted in Unreliable Estimates, Partly Due to its Failure to Follow Best Practices and Guidelines for Federal Statistical Agencies

We found several issues with BEA's methodology that resulted in unreliable remittance estimates. BEA also did not follow its own best practices and Office of Management and Budget (OMB) or NRC guidance on documentation and methods for analysis that could have ensured reliability of its methodology and limited the inaccuracy in its estimates.

BEA Did Not Follow Its Own Best Practices for Documenting Its Procedures

Despite OMB and agency guidance and best practices that would provide that BEA should document its procedures for developing its new model for estimating remittances, BEA did not prepare adequate, transparent documentation of its efforts to develop its new model. BEA also did not prepare adequate documentation of management review and approval of the new model.

OMB's Information Quality Act (IQA) guidelines, which are designed so that agencies will meet basic information quality standards, state that agencies should ensure that data and methods are documented and transparent enough to allow an independent reanalysis by a qualified member of the public.[37] IQA guidelines also direct agencies to develop management procedures for reviewing and substantiating the quality of information before it is disseminated. According to BEA best practice guidance, all changes in either methodology or data sources should receive documented management approval.[38]

In its own internal guidelines, BEA notes that it strives for the highest level of transparency about data and methods for its estimates to support the development of high-quality data and facilitate efforts to reproduce the information. Additionally, BEA best practices guidelines are designed to ensure the accuracy of input data; provide high-quality, timely analyses that document how estimates are made; and provide estimates that satisfy both internal and external customer needs. One BEA best practice is to enhance both transparency and replicability by instructing BEA staff to document each step or change in the methodology and document the rationale behind each decision.[39] Another BEA best practice states that written analyses of the estimate should include a discussion of changes and revisions as well as deviations from standard methods. However, based on our analysis, BEA did not follow these guidelines, as the following examples illustrate.

- Documentation showing how the final remittance estimate is calculated was not maintained. When asked to provide records of analysis that supported the calculations of 2012 and 2013 remittance estimates (the most recent estimates available at the time of our review), BEA staff told us that the documents were created only when each year's estimate was produced and were not saved. Unable to produce its original documents, BEA recreated the documentation to fulfill our request. However, BEA staff told us that the file could be missing some information required to successfully run the computer program that calculates total remittance estimates; for example, certain variables had been renamed and some fields were missing; their numbers were also multiplied by an arbitrary discount factor whose use was explained to us only later as something done to avoid a break in the series.[40]
- Changes and revisions were not sufficiently documented. When asked to provide documentation of the analyses completed to determine changes in the model, BEA provided a conference paper containing written descriptions of its regression analyses.[41] BEA staff who completed these analyses told us that the regression files had not been saved in a way that would allow the staff to easily provide us with the files applicable to the model changes. The staff described saving them among many partially complete files and told us that it would be difficult to identify the files that led to the current version of the model. Unable to provide its original research, BEA attempted to recreate the steps that were used to create the model.[42]
- Management review of estimation methodology was insufficiently documented. BEA officials noted that staff adhered to internal guidance by obtaining both managerial and external reviews of the model's revision but provided little documentation of them. BEA staff said the remittance model proposal was presented to the

Modernization and Enhancement Steering Committee (MESC) for formal review.[43] BEA provided minutes of the MESC meeting discussing the review of the model, but the minutes also indicated that BEA management was still considering changes. BEA staff could not provide documentation of additional management actions taken or of another MESC meeting held at a later date. BEA staff told us that the agency subjected the output of research that affected methodology changes to a full gamut of validity checks. However, the only documentation we received of a validity test was the MESC meeting minutes that contained a discussion of the model's assumptions. BEA staff told us that the personal transfers model had been subjected to additional scrutiny by BEA senior management resulting from the authors' conference presentations.[44] However, BEA did not provide us with either documentation of the conference feedback or the results of senior management's additional scrutiny. BEA officials stated that the decision to publish a Survey of Current Business article about the model's revision constituted verification of management review.[45] However, BEA could not provide any documentation of the approval process for publication to demonstrate what the management review entailed.

- The rationale and appropriateness of its methodology for estimating remittances was not documented. According to NRC guidelines for federal statistical agencies data releases from a statistical program should be accompanied by assumptions used for data collection, and what is known about the quality and relevance of the data.[46] The guidelines also mention appropriate methods for analysis that take account of variability and other sources of error and the results of research on the methods and data. We found BEA did not follow these guidelines, as illustrated by the following examples,
- Data. We were unable to verify the accuracy of the data because we were not provided with documents detailing the steps and analyses BEA undertook to convert CPS data to the dataset BEA actually used to estimate the model. A BEA best practice states that an analysis of the estimate should include a discussion of questionable aspects of the source data, including outliers.[47] However, BEA could not provide us with documents showing analyses performed to deal with various problematic aspects of the data and treatment of outliers.[48] In addition, BEA conducts an analysis to assign a portion of the household's income to each individual in the household. The income amount

attributed to each individual is a critical component of the model and has a substantial effect on the result, yet BEA could not provide any documents showing sensitivity analyses of this critical assumption to see how the attribution of income affects its results.[49] Further, for some households that did not have any family income in CPS data, BEA assigned them incomes but could not tell us how they calculated them. BEA also assigned all households within a given range of family income the same income.[50] This approach introduces measurement error to the extent that households within a given range of family income do not, in fact, have the same income. BEA could not provide any documentation explaining these details or what implications the assigned incomes could have on its results.

- Estimation Technique. As described earlier, BEA used a nonstandard iterative technique to estimate its model. BEA staff acknowledged that the method was unusual and may be hard to comprehend. When we requested additional information on management review of the model, BEA staff stated that they had had the model reviewed by an outside expert. However, officials later said the review was informal and no written opinion was provided.[51]
- Model specification. BEA did not follow IMF's guide for compilers in two instances related to issues of model specification.[52] First, the guide specifies that the variables used to explain and predict remittance rates may need to be converted to different forms to see if they generate a better model.[53] BEA could provide no documentation showing it attempted to do this analysis. Second, the IMF guide states that statistical analyses are also needed to understand the relationship of different demographic variables to each other and to remittance rates in order to select the relevant variables. BEA could not provide us with any documentation showing they performed any tests on the relationship among different demographic variables.
- Goodness-of-fit. This term refers to how well a model represents the data.[54] The IMF guide states that various statistics describing goodness-of-fit should be calculated to decide on the best model for determining the level of remittances. BEA presented the results of only one such test, namely the "R-squared (R2)."[55] Moreover, BEA does not report standard errors for their models' coefficients using their iterative method and does not document that this iterative method would produce correct standard errors for these coefficients.[56]

BEA's Methodology Resulted in Unreliable Estimates

We identified several errors in BEA's analysis that led us to question the reliability of BEA's estimates. Moreover, BEA adjusted the new model to match results from its prior model, contributing to inaccuracy in its estimates. We found the following problems with BEA's methodology.

- Presence of outliers in the data had a substantial influence on the model's results. There are 6,136 households in BEA's data. In its data, the CPS reported that 51 households (0.9 percent of all households) remitted $27,199. The CPS averages remittances across all households that remit more than $10,000 annually and assigns the average (in this case, $27,199) to each of these households. BEA includes these 51 households in its data, all of which are assumed by BEA to remit $27,199 even though they differ in income levels. These households are outliers in BEA's data, since all other households included remit between $0 and $10,000. These outliers are highly influential, as excluding them significantly changes the remittance rates that would have resulted using BEA's own methodology. For example, BEA calculates that a person who is married with a spouse absent, lives with roommates, has been in the United States for less than 5 years, and belongs to the highest country tier remits 73.1 percent of his or her income (see table 1).[57] If we remove the outliers from the data, this percentage changes to 14.9 percent. OMB's Statistical Policy Directive No. 1 states that where appropriate any known or potential data limitations or sources of error should be described to data users so they can evaluate the suitability of the data for a particular purpose.[58] But BEA does not mention this aspect of the data in its publication even though it has significant influence on the results.
- BEA's model was not consistent with the data. BEA's model assumption that all individuals within a demographic category remit on average the same percentage of their income is inconsistent with its data, which show that 75 percent of households remit nothing at all. Moreover, BEA's model generates remittance rates for certain categories of households that have no individuals in them. For example, the model calculates that individuals in households with married persons with absent spouses who have roommates, who remit to low-tier countries, and who have spent 6 to 15 years in the United States,

remit 8.5 percent of their income. However, there are no such individuals in the data.[59] BEA failed to point out these data deficiencies even though OMB's Statistical Policy Directive No.4 asks agencies to clearly point out limitations of the data to users.[60]

Table 1. Remittance Rates from Bureau of Economic Analysis's Model, with and without Outliers

		With outliers[a]			Without outliers[b]		
Country tier	Family structure	0 to 5 years	6 to 15 years	15 plus years	0 to 5 years	6 to 15 years	15 plus years
Low	Other marital, no roommates	1.1%	0.8%	0.5%	0.4%	0.3%	0.2%
Low	Other marital, with roommates	3.9	2.9	1.6	0.8	0.7	0.3
Low	MSA, no roommates	5.9	4.5	2.4	1.6	1.4	0.7
Low	MSA, with roommates	11.2	8.5	4.6	1.4	1.2	0.6
Middle	Other marital, no roommates	1.1	0.8	0.5	1.2	1.0	0.5
Middle	Other marital, with roommates	3.9	2.9	1.6	2.5	2.2	1.0
Middle	MSA, no roommates	5.9	4.5	2.4	5.0	4.3	2.1
Middle	MSA, with roommates	11.1	8.5	4.6	4.3	3.7	1.8
High	Other marital, no roommates	2.8	2.1	1.1	2.0	1.7	0.8
High	Other marital, with roommates	9.7	7.3	4.0	4.1	3.5	1.7
High	MSA, no roommates	14.8	11.2	6.1	8.2	7.0	3.4
High	MSA, with roommates	28.0	21.2	11.5	7.0	6.0	2.9
Highest	Other marital, no roommates	7.2	5.5	3.0	4.2	3.6	1.7
Highest	Other marital, with roommates	25.4	19.2	10.4	8.8	7.5	3.6
Highest	MSA, no roommates	38.6	29.3	15.9	17.5	14.9	7.2
Highest	MSA, with roommates	73.1	55.5	30.1	14.9	12.7	6.1

Legend: MSA = married, spouse absent.
Source: BEA and GAO calculations | GAO-16-60
Notes: Outliers consist of those remitting over $10,000 but being assigned a value of $27,199. Out of 6,136 households, 51 outliers were removed for this comparison.
[a]Rates provided by BEA.
[b]GAO calculation using BEA methodology after removing the outliers from the dataset.

- Failure to account for censored data leads to biased results. Because the value of reported remittances is only partially known, BEA's remittance data are censored data. The remittance data are censored (at the bottom) because 75 percent of households remit $0 and all other households remit positive sums. The remittance data are censored (at the top) because, as noted earlier, the CPS assigns all households that remit over $10,000 a remittance value of $27,199. Estimating a model on censored data demands certain econometric techniques, which BEA has not adopted, in order to yield unbiased estimates.[61] The guidelines presented by NRC as mentioned above specifically ask agencies to use appropriate methods for analysis that take account of variability and other sources of error.[62]
- BEA's model is incorrectly specified in its documentation, and the actual model specification may lead to biases. BEA's documentation states that its model explains the total amount remitted by a household (in part) in terms of that household's income level. However, BEA's model assumes that the total amount remitted by a household depends only on the income of the foreign-born individuals in the household.[63] To the extent that U.S.-born individuals in a household do remit, BEA's model overestimates the fraction of income remitted by foreign-born individuals in that household. BEA officials said that they excluded U.S.-born individuals from a household on the basis that they remitted very little. But we found that 407 households with only U.S.-born individuals reported remitting almost 13 percent of total remittances, suggesting that the remittance rates of foreign-born individuals may be overestimated and, thus, biased.
- Measurement errors in a critical explanatory variable bias the results. As explained earlier, BEA's assignment of household income to individuals within the household is critical to its analysis. Since this individual income variable is subject to measurement error, it biases the effect of this variable on the remittance rates, contributing to the unreliability of the remittance estimates calculated by BEA.
- Several coding and other errors also contributed to inaccuracy. BEA staff said that they considered the estimation of the personal transfers model a relatively straightforward task.[64] As such, they did not consider independent programming of code by a reviewer necessary. We found several errors and unexplained adjustments in BEA's code that might have been detected had a review been conducted.

- Calibration of this new model to match unreliable old estimates enhanced unreliability. BEA's model predicts total remittance amounts that are substantially lower than those BEA has historically published. BEA handles this difference by multiplying the remittance rates from its model by an arbitrary calibration factor so that the total model's estimated remittances equal those that BEA previously calculated for 2008.[65] BEA calibrated the model because an analysis of CPS data determined that remittance rates may have been underestimated because many immigrants were reluctant to report their precise remittances.[66] Because BEA calibrated the new model to old estimates, BEA estimated the same remittance amount for the year 2008 that the old model had produced. For the years following 2008, the remittance estimates differed slightly from the previous estimates because of the different demographic characteristics used in the new model (see table 2).

Table 2. Comparison of Estimates from BEA's Old and New Methodologies

Dollars in billions		
	Totalannual remittances	
	Old methodology	**New methodology**
2001	$26.5	$27.1
2002	27.7	27.4
2003	28.0	27.5
2004	30.4	30.1
2005	31.3	30.9
2006	34.3	35.3
2007	36.9	37.1
2008	38.5	38.5
2009	37.4	36.1
2010	37.1	35.6

Source: GAO analysis of BEA data. | GAO-16-60.

In our March 2006 report on BEA remittance estimates, we questioned the accuracy of BEA estimates based on the model developed in 2005 after finding that the remittance rates BEA used were primarily based on its own judgment.[67] We found shortcomings in BEA's model, specifically with regard to the assumptions BEA made about the percentage of income remitted and the percentage of foreign-born persons who remit. We were unable to link the parameters that BEA used to capture the remitting behavior of foreign-born persons directly to the sources that BEA cited. We found that BEA used its own judgment to determine the proportion of the adult foreign-born population that sent remittances and the proportion of income they remitted. We concluded that the accuracy of these estimates was affected both by the quality of the underlying data as well as by these assumptions. Therefore, calibration of the new model—which may itself be unreliable—to the old estimates further affects the reliability of the final estimates.

BEA Does Not Regard Its Remittance Estimate as Influential

BEA officials told us that the personal transfers estimate was not a principal economic indicator. Therefore, BEA considered information related to the development of the estimate to be influential (as defined by OMB's IQA guidelines) only in terms of the integrity of the estimate's dissemination.[68] Nonetheless, BEA's Information Quality Guidelines state that at BEA the notion of data integrity goes beyond the maintaining of the security of its information. Integrity includes, among other things, transparency that is ensured by providing certain information, such as assumptions for missing source data and discussions of revisions.[69] BEA officials also noted that personal remittances were a relatively small component of the U.S. current account.[70] According to BEA officials, over the past 5 years personal transfers accounted for an average of 0.59 percent of gross current account transactions. Officials said that, as a result, resources devoted to improving the estimation of personal remittances had to be balanced with resources allocated to improving other estimates that could be more important to the balance of payments. However, a number of organizations use BEA's estimates. BEA reports its personal transfer estimates to IMF, which publishes country estimates in its Balance of Payments Statistics Yearbook. In addition, the World Bank uses BEA estimates submitted to IMF as part of its calculations on remittances. IDB's Multilateral Investment Fund also uses estimates published by IMF as a baseline for its calculations of individual country estimates.

BEA officials also noted that OMB's guidelines give agencies discretion in determining the level of quality to which information will be held.[71] However, while the guidelines do afford agencies some discretion, the guidelines make it clear that agencies should not disseminate substantive information that does not meet a basic level of quality.[72] As discussed earlier, by failing to follow its best practices, BEA has not met this basic quality level.

BEA officials did not explain the reasons behind not following their own best practices or failing to maintain adequate documentation along the way. We have previously stated that appropriate documentation of a significant event or internal control, in a manner that allows it to be readily available for examination, is an example of a control activity that can be taken by federal program management.[73] This type of control activity allows management to achieve objectives and respond to risks in its internal control system. Such events would include supervisory review of methodological changes to BEA's estimation model.

Moreover, BEA's best practices require documentation of its methodology and data and supervisory and management review and approval of any changes. But BEA has not provided sufficient and transparent documentation of its procedures for developing its new personal remittance estimation model. The lack of documentation made our evaluation of BEA's model and estimates difficult, and it was not possible for us to obtain reasonable assurance that BEA met federal guidelines and its own internal standards. Because the documentation provided to us by BEA is lacking in both clarity and completeness, we cannot say that BEA has met the goal of IQA to ensure and maximize the quality, objectivity, utility, and integrity of its remittance statistics, which are public information disseminated by federal agencies. However, based on the information we were able to obtain, we were still able to determine that the model produces unreliable annual estimates.

CONCLUSION

BEA's updated model for estimating remittances produces unreliable results due to underlying issues with the data, such as missing information and measurement problems. BEA did not satisfactorily explain why its methodology was appropriate, despite NRC's guidance to do so. Moreover, BEA calibrated the new estimates to align with those from its old model, the accuracy of which we had previously called into question. Additionally, BEA could not provide us with sufficient documentation of the steps it took to test the model and ensure it received management review and approval—key quality assurance procedures.

Documentation of BEA's processes of analyzing, testing, and reviewing its model should not be simply an act of memorializing events. Documentation also provides evidence of an agency's adherence to procedures and policies that are part of its quality assurance framework. BEA's methodology for estimating remittances is not consistent with guidelines prescribed by BEA's best practices standards, the standards of IQA, OMB statistical directives, and NRC guidance. Had BEA subjected its model to these standards, it would have taken important steps toward obtaining reasonable assurance that it had produced reliable annual estimates of remittances.

Although BEA officials discount the importance of remittances as a component of international transactions statistics, the inability of BEA's new model to produce more accurate remittances estimates is consequential, as BEA's estimate is the official remittance estimate of the United States and is cited by both national and international organizations, and in some cases incorporated into the estimates of these organizations.

RECOMMENDATIONS FOR EXECUTIVE ACTION

We recommend that the Secretary of Commerce direct the BEA Director to take the following actions:

To improve the reliability of the annual official U.S. estimate of remittances, conduct additional analyses of BEA's estimates using estimation techniques appropriate for dealing with the shortcomings of the data. Analyses should also be conducted to understand the effect of various assumptions behind and limitations of the data on the estimates.

To improve the transparency and quality of BEA's international remittances estimate, follow established BEA best practices, OMB policies, and NRC guidance for documenting BEA's methods and analyses used to revise its model for estimating remittances and for producing its annual estimates.

AGENCY COMMENTS AND OUR EVALUATION

We provided a draft of this report to the Secretaries of Commerce, Homeland Security, State and the Treasury, the Chair of the Board of Governors of the Federal Reserve System, and the Director of Consumer Financial Protection Bureau (CFPB). Commerce provided a letter, including written comments from the Bureau of Economic Analysis (BEA) on a draft of the report. CFPB, Treasury and State provided technical comments, which we incorporated as appropriate.

In its comment letter, BEA stated that it intends to implement our two recommendations to the extent possible consistent with resource limitations as it continuously improves its remittance (personal transfer) estimate and other estimates. However, BEA stated that it did not agree with our report's conclusions that its remittance estimates are unreliable or that its documentation of changes to its estimation model or annual estimates is inadequate. More specifically, BEA commented that it believes that its remittance estimates are valid and reasonable for the purpose for which they are prepared and that the documentation provided to GAO was fully adequate. We recognize BEA's resource constraints. However, we maintain that our findings related to the reliability of BEA's remittance estimates and documentation of the methodology to produce such estimates are valid and support the recommendations we made in the report.

Regarding our conclusion that BEA's remittance estimates are unreliable, in its comment letter BEA acknowledged the data limitations that GAO pointed out in the report but did not explain how these may affect its estimates. The limitations described in BEA's comment letter were not discussed in the documentation provided by BEA. Nor did BEA provide evidence showing that it conducted alternative analyses to conclude that these limitations did not affect the quality of its final estimates. For example, in its comment letter BEA mentions that the calculation of its income variable was problematic but during our review did not present us with analysis to show how sensitive its estimates were to various assumptions about income, including that of taking the midpoint of the range of income provided in its data. Even BEA's choice of demographic variables included in their analysis depends on how it calculates individual income. BEA acknowledges that its data was censored—where the value of reported remittances for some households in its data set is only partially known—but during our review, it did not provide evidence that it conducted additional analyses using an alternative methodology to see how final estimates might be affected. BEA told us that these households were responsible for a substantial proportion of all remittances and we found that it had considerable influence on BEA's estimates. Though these and other data limitations described in this report could have substantial impact on the estimates, in its comments BEA dismisses the limitations stating that they would only have marginal effect on the estimates. However, BEA does not present evidence of having tested the magnitude of the effects on the estimates. Moreover, calibrating the estimates resulting from BEA's revised estimation model to its previous estimates, the accuracy of which was deemed uncertain in a previous GAO report, further undermines our confidence in these estimates. As a result of data limitations, BEA's choice of methodology in light of those limitations, and other errors and corrections BEA made, we maintain that BEA's revised estimation model produces unreliable remittance estimates.

Regarding our conclusion that BEA did not follow the best practices, policies, and guidance to which it is subject for documenting its methods and analyses, BEA stated that the documentation provided to GAO was fully adequate. We disagree. As discussed in this report, we identified several instances where BEA did not follow best practices, policies, and guidance. For example, we requested files that provided documentation of the analyses BEA conducted to determine changes to its estimation methodology. BEA provided written descriptions of its regression analysis in a conference paper. BEA staff told us that its analysis files had been saved among many partially complete files and that it would be difficult to identify the files that led to the current version of the model. BEA's best practice standards require that all methodological changes and the rationale for the changes be clearly documented. As we describe in the report, without documentation BEA could not effectively convey and support the rationale and appropriateness of its methodology. We were unable to verify, among other things, the accuracy of much of BEA's data or fully understand the selection of its methodology.

As we stated in the report, documentation of analysis, testing, and evaluations of models should show evidence of adherence to procedures and policies that are part of an effective quality assurance framework. BEA did not provide documentation that reflected such a framework. For example, BEA officials described conducting managerial and external reviews of the model's revision but provided only the minutes to one management review meeting indicating that the model had been discussed but was still under consideration. Though we requested documentation of final approval of the model by the management committee, BEA told us that it had nothing further to provide. BEA also described an external review of its model revision that was done by an external econometrician for quality assurance purposes. When we asked for documentation of this review, however, BEA told us that it had been informal and that no written opinion had been provided.

In addition, BEA stated that our ability to reproduce the agency's estimates showed that its documentation was adequate. However, we did not attempt to reproduce BEA's estimates. Rather, we ran the computer program that BEA provided on the data created by BEA to replicate a few intermediate steps in its methodology. By replicating these steps, we found inconsistencies between BEA's description of the analysis and what was actually done, and other errors. We did not and would not have been able to reproduce the analysis, based on the documentation that BEA provided, that led to the final remittance estimates or even create the dataset used by BEA from its listed sources.

BEA noted that it provided us with new summaries to help explain certain aspects of its methodology, but asserted that we conflated this additional effort with an inadequacy of internal control and initial documentation. However, we maintain that in some cases, BEA provided these summaries because it was unable to provide us with original documentation. For example, we asked for records of analysis that supported the calculations of 2012 and 2013 estimates. BEA told us that the documents were created only when each year's estimate was produced and were not saved. BEA also was unable to provide original documentation of the analysis that led to the current version of the model and attempted to recreate its steps in new documentation.

BEA also rejected the statement that it did not follow best practices because it did not consider remittances to be influential. During our review, BEA staff told us that information about BEA's remittance estimates was designated as influential only to prevent their disclosure before they were officially released. BEA also told us orally and in writing that as personal remittances were a relatively small component of the U.S. current account, resources devoted to improving the estimate of remittances had to be balanced with resources allocated to improving other estimates that could be more important to the balance of payments.

Finally, BEA stated its remittance estimate was not designed to measure the potential impact of the WIRE Act (proposed Remittance Status Verification Act of 2015), and it understood that we would use its estimates as a basis for understanding the magnitude of cross-border transfers. BEA's comment inaccurately described the purpose and scope of our review. As we describe in this report, our review focused on two separate objectives which were to (1) discuss the potential effects of assessing a fine on remitters unable to provide proof of legal U.S. immigration status, and (2) examine BEA's remittance estimate and the extent to which its revised estimation methodology met government-wide policies and agency best practices. We used information on BEA's remittance estimates solely to help us answer the report's second objective.

Alicia Puente Cackley
Director,
Financial Markets and Community Investment

Appendix I: Objectives, Scope, and Methodology

This report (1) discusses the potential effects of collecting information from and imposing a fine on remitters unable to provide proof of legal U.S. immigration status, and (2) examines the Bureau of Economic Analysis' (BEA) remittance estimate and the extent to which the revised estimation methodology met government-wide policies and agency best practices.

To discuss the potential effects of assessing a fine on remitters unable to provide proof of U.S. immigration status, we summarized estimates of the number of immigrants without legal status from federal agencies and research organizations, including the Department of Homeland Security (DHS), Pew Research Center, and Center for Migration Studies (CMS). Together, DHS, Pew Research, and CMS are primary sources for the estimates of immigrants without legal status in the United States, which we determined by asking experts from each organization above to discuss all other similar estimates. Through interviews with immigration researchers, review of research articles, and comparison of the estimates, which ranged from 11.1 million to 11.4 million immigrants in the United States without legal status in 2012, we determined that the estimates were authoritative and sufficiently reliable for the purposes of this report. We used these sources to identify the size of the potentially affected group of immigrants without legal status.

To acquire information on the effects of the proposed requirement to provide proof of legal status or pay a fine, we reviewed relevant academic and industry studies based on a literature search. We reviewed and summarized the literature for factors that could be associated with the proposed legislation, including the number and remitting behavior of immigrants without legal status, changes in remittance flows in response to a price increase, the effect of requiring proof of legal status on remittances, and market competition between remittance providers.. We determined the studies to be reliable for our purposes.

To obtain perspectives on the potential effects of imposing a fine on remitters without proof of U.S. legal status, we interviewed researchers with expertise in remittances and immigration to the United States, financial institutions, remittance service providers, two industry trade associations, one state audit association, two community groups with knowledge of remitters' concerns, and knowledgeable federal and international agencies. We judgmentally selected a cross-section of remittance transfer providers that included five nondepository remittance transfer providers and four depository institutions based on a number of factors, including the volume of remittances and diversity of countries serviced. We spoke with regulators, including the Consumer Financial Protection Bureau (CFPB) and the Financial Crimes Enforcement Network (FinCEN), to obtain their perspectives on compliance with requirements of the proposed Remittance Status Verification Act of 2015, should it become law. We also reviewed laws and regulations relevant to remittance transfer providers. Researchers with expertise in remittance transfers were selected by contacting two recognized experts and asking for referrals. We interviewed the experts recommended and continued to ask for others until the referrals began to repeat with experts we already interviewed. To select community groups, we asked others we interviewed for recommended groups.

To highlight the uncertainty associated with the effects of the fine, we constructed a scenario analysis of several factors that may affect net revenue from the fine, which is the amount of fine collected that remains available for border protection after payment of CFPB's administrative and enforcements costs. We varied hypothetical amounts for the following three factors: dollar amount of remittances sent by immigrants without legal status, the percentage reduction in remittances in response to the fine, and the cost for administration and enforcement. We selected the three factors by analyzing them among other potential factors and we found that these three provided wide variability in net revenue from the fine. Other factors we considered included the volume of total remittances, the percentage transmitted through formal methods, and the percent of remittances sent by immigrants without legal status. Though we conducted a literature search for statistics for each factor in our analysis, any studies found were not generalizable or sufficient for our purposes. The data were limited to remittance flows between specific countries, for example remittances sent between the United States and Mexico, or were not recent. Therefore, the dollar amounts or percentages given to each factor in our scenario analysis are hypothetical and selected only to show the potential variability in net revenue from the fine.

To obtain information on BEA's estimate of remittances (personal transfers) from the United States, we met several times with BEA officials responsible for developing the estimate. They provided us with an estimate of the total volume of remittances from the United States to the rest of the world from 2006 to 2014 that they provided to the IMF for inclusion in balance of payments statistics. In this report, we further assess BEA's estimation model and find that its results are unreliable.

To understand BEA's revised methodology for estimating remittances (personal transfers) we conducted multiple interviews with BEA staff responsible for developing the estimate. We obtained BEA documentation describing the agency's approach to estimating remittances, including components of its model, related statistical program files, and its outputs. We reviewed BEA's presentation and description of the model and checked for consistency with its statistical program files and other calculations. We provided BEA with numerous follow-up questions about the methodology, and BEA provided us with written responses and attended additional meetings to provide more clarity. We also obtained documentation on the Census Bureau's (Census) American Community Survey and Current Population Survey data to understand how they were used in BEA's remittance estimation methodology and interviewed Census officials familiar with the survey. We also reviewed BEA's best practices, Office of Management and Budget (OMB) statistical directives, and the National Research Council (NRC) of the National Academies of Sciences' manual for statistical agencies to determine the extent to which BEA's methodological changes conformed with guidance on statistical practices.

To determine the extent to which BEA documented its changed methodology and its results and adhered to best practice standards, we met with BEA staff responsible for developing the estimate. BEA staff explained their documentation procedures to us. BEA staff also provided copies of BEA guidance on best practices regarding methodological changes. We also reviewed relevant law and regulations, as well as guidance from IMF, the Department of Commerce, OMB, and NRC. We reviewed documents provided by BEA for transparency and completeness. Additionally, we provided BEA with follow-up questions about the agency's documentation processes and procedures, and BEA provided us with written responses. After receiving the responses, we again met with BEA staff to discuss these processes and procedures.

To obtain a variety of views on remittance estimation, we met with officials from IMF, World Bank, Inter-American Development Bank and their external consultant, as well as the Mexican and Philippine central banks. We selected these two countries because they were among the top 10 recipient countries of U.S. annual outflows and both countries use a formal methodology to track inflows and outflows on at least an annual basis. In meetings with these entities, we gained an understanding of the methodologies used to estimate remittances and challenges in remittance estimation.

We conducted this performance audit from October 2014 to February 2016 in accordance with generally accepted government auditing standards. Those standards require that we plan and perform the audit to obtain sufficient, appropriate evidence to provide a reasonable basis for our findings and conclusions based on our audit objectives. We believe that the evidence obtained provides a reasonable basis for our findings and conclusions based on our audit objectives.

End Notes

[1] The World Bank, *World Development Indicators: Movement of People Across Borders,* 2014. The World Bank defines personal remittances as the sum of personal transfers and compensation of employees. Personal transfers represent all current transfers in cash or in kind made between resident and nonresident individuals. Compensation of employees represents the income of border, seasonal, and other short-term workers who are employed in an economy where they are not residents and of residents employed by nonresident entities.

[2] GAO, *International Remittances: Different Estimation Methodologies Produce Different Results*, GAO-06-210 (Washington, D.C.: March 2006).

[3] The Group of Eight is a governmental political forum of industrial economies, including Canada, France, Germany, Italy, Japan, the United States, and the United Kingdom, as well as other countries in the European Union.

[4] International Monetary Fund, *International transactions in remittances: guide for compilers and users* (Washington, D.C.: 2009).

[5] S. 79, 114th Cong. (1st Sess. 2015).

[6] In 2010, the Dodd-Frank Wall Street Reform and Consumer Protection Act (Dodd-Frank Act) amended EFTA to add a new legal framework for remittance transfers. Pub. L. No. 111-203, § 1073, 124 Stat. 1376, 2060 (2010) (codified at 15 U.S.C. § 1693o-1). The Dodd-Frank Act also transferred most rulemaking authority, including that related to remittance transfers, under EFTA from the Board of Governors of the Federal Reserve (Federal Reserve Board) to the Consumer Financial Protection Bureau (CFPB). CFPB amended Regulation E, under EFTA, to implement the requirements for remittance transfers. Regulation E requires remittance transfer providers to make certain disclosures to senders of remittance transfers, including, among other things, a pre-payment disclosure containing such information as fees, taxes and exchange rates. 12 C.F.R. § 1005.31(b). Regulation E also includes specific procedures to be followed in the event of an error. *See* 12 C.F.R. § 1005.33. A remittance transfer provider is generally defined as any person that provides remittance transfers for a consumer in the normal course of its business, regardless of whether the consumer holds an account with such person. *See* 12 C.F.R. § 1005.30(f). A remittance transfer is generally defined as the electronic transfer of funds requested by a sender (defined as a consumer in a state who primarily for personal, family, or household purposes requests a remittance transfer provider to send a remittance transfer) to a designated recipient that is sent by a remittance transfer provider, and does not include transfers in the amount of $15 or less among other exclusions. 12 C.F.R. § 1005.30(e).

[7] A Matrícula Consular de Alta Seguridad (Consular Identification Card), issued by the Government of Mexico to its nationals residing outside of Mexico, would not constitute acceptable documentation under the proposed law.

[8] See Phillip Conner, D'Vera Cohn, Ana Gonzalez-Barrerra, and Russ Oates, *Changing Patterns of Global Migration and Remittances* (Washington, D.C.: Pew Research Center, 2013).

[9] United States Census, *Selected Characteristics of the Native and Foreign-Born Populations, 2010-2014, American Community Survey 5-year Estimates*, accessed December, 11, 2015, http://factfinder.census.gov/faces/tableservices/jsf/pages/productview.xhtml?pid=ACS_14_1YR_S0501&prodType=table.

[10] We discussed the oversight and supervision of banks and nonbank remittance transfer providers, as it relates to anti-money-laundering requirements, in a recently issued report. See GAO, *International Remittances: Money Laundering Risks and Views on Enhanced Customer Verification and Recordkeeping Requirements*, GAO-16-65 (Washington, D.C.: Jan.15, 2016).

[11] Hawalas make up an informal value transfer system for transferring money that is often used in places where formal financial transactions are unavailable, expensive, or unreliable. Senders pay money to an agent, who then instructs a remote associate to pay the final recipient.

[12] The sixth edition of the *Balance of Payments and International Investment Position Manual* serves as the standard framework for statistics on the transactions between a country's economy and the rest of the world.

[13] The data published by the World Bank is not fully consistent with the *Balance of Payments and International Investment Position Manual*, and therefore, caution should be taken in comparing different data sets. The World Bank's most recent official data on remittances and other resources are available at http://www.worldbank.org/en/topic/migration remittancesdiasporaissues/brief/migrationremittances-data.

[14] International Monetary Fund, *International transactions in remittances: guide for compilers and users* (Washington, D.C.: 2009).

[15] The guide defines net compensation of employees as the compensation of employees less (1) taxes and social contributions paid by nonresident workers in the economy of employment and (2) transport and travel expenditures related to working abroad.

[16] See Jeffrey S. Passel and D'Vera Cohn, *Unauthorized Immigrant Totals Rise in 7 States, Fall in 14* (Washington: D.C: Pew Research Center, 2014); Bryan Baker and Nancy Rytina, *Estimates of the Unauthorized Immigrant Population Residing in the United States*, Population Estimates, Policy Directorate (Washington, D.C.: U.S. Department of Homeland Security, Office of Immigration Statistics, 2013); and Robert Warren, "Democratizing Data about Unauthorized Residents in the United States: Estimates and Public-Use Data, 2010-2013," *Journal on Migration and Human Security*, vol. 2, no. 4 (Center for Migration Studies, 2014), 305-328. More recent estimates of unauthorized residents in the United States are available from the Pew Research Center and the Center for Migration Studies, which report 11.3 million and 10.9 million in 2014, respectively. See Jeffrey S. Passel and D'Vera Cohn, Unauthorized Immigrant Population Stable for Half a Decade (Washington, D.C: Pew Research Center, 2015), accessed on February 9, 2016, http://www.pewresearch.org/fact-tank/2015/07/22/unauthorized-immigrant-population-stable-for-half-a-decade/; and Robert Warren, "US Undocumented Population Drops Below 11 Million in 2014, with Continued Declines in the Mexican Undocumented Population," *Journal on Migration and Human Security*, vol. 4, no. 1 (Center for Migration Studies, 2016), 1-15.

[17] For information on the use of informal networks by immigrants without legal status, see Catalina Amuedo-Dorantes, Cynthia Bansak, and Susan Pozo, "On the Remitting Patterns of Immigrants: Evidence from Mexican Survey Data," *Economic Review*, Federal Reserve Bank of Atlanta, vol. 90, no. 1 (2005); and Raúl Hernández Coss, "The U.S.–Mexico

Remittance Corridor: Lessons on Shifting from Informal to Formal Transfer Systems" (working paper, Series No. 47, Washington, D.C.: 2005).

[18] For example, one researcher suggested that if individuals are willing to cross the border without legal status, then they might be willing to use transfer systems that are not regulated. Similarly, two articles from our review of the literature suggest that not having legal status may also raise the demand for informal transfer services, given a desire to remain in the country undetected by public authorities. On the other hand, transferring money safely to family members abroad may be so important that immigrants may send money using regulated providers, even if doing so results in higher costs. AmuedoDorantes, Bansak, and Pozo, "On the Remitting Patterns of Immigrants: Evidence from Mexican Survey Data," and Hernández-Coss, "The U.S.–Mexico Remittance Corridor Lessons on Shifting from Informal to Formal Transfer Systems."

[19] For example, our search of the literature found one study on price sensitivity for remittances from the United States, which was limited to remittances sent to El Salvador and Guatemala. With regard to the likelihood of remittances, one study of Mexican migrants finds that unauthorized immigrants are more likely to remit, while another study of African migrants to Organization for Economic Co-operation and Development countries finds that unauthorized migrants are less likely to remit. For the study on price sensitivity, see Kate Ambler, Diego Aycinena, and Dean Yang, "Remittance Responses to Temporary Discounts: A Field Experiment Among Central American Migrants" (working paper 20522, Massachusetts, National Bureau of Economic Research, 2014). For the study on whether migrants from Mexico without legal status are more likely to remit, see Amuedo-Dorantes, Bansak, and Pozo, "On the Remitting Patterns of Immigrants: Evidence from Mexican Survey Data." And for the contribution of legal status on remittances by African migrants, see Albert Bollard, David McKenzie, and Melanie Morten, "The Remitting Patterns of African Migrants in the OECD," (working paper 5260, Washington, D.C.: World Bank, April 2010).

[20] Consumer Financial Protection Bureau, *Report on remittance transfers: Report to the President, the Senate Committee on Banking, Housing, and Urban Affairs, and the House of Representatives Committee on Financial Services* (Washington, D.C.: 2011).

[21] Because it would amend EFTA, the proposed legislation would fall under the supervision and enforcement authority of other federal regulators, in addition to CFPB, depending on the institution being supervised or enforced against. CFPB generally has the authority to supervise very large banks and credit unions, as well as certain nonbank entities (including those currently defined by rule to be nonbank international money transfer providers that send at least one million international money transfers annually), for compliance with federal consumer financial law, including EFTA. Enforcement authority under EFTA depends on the institution. *See* 15 U.S.C. § 1693o(a). The proposed legislation, however, does not provide that any funds obtained from the fine would go to any of the other federal regulators.

[22] If CFPB incurred expenses that do not reduce proportionately with the volume of remittances, or the percentage of remittances not sent through regulated providers, then net revenue might be negative. For example, if the costs for rulemaking were large and subtracted from CFPBs expenses in the first year of implementation, then net revenue might be negative for that year.

[23] Other regulators with enforcement authority under EFTA include the National Credit Union Administration, the Federal Reserve Board, Office of the Comptroller of the Currency,

Federal Deposit Insurance Corporation, the Department of Transportation, and the Securities and Exchange Commission. *See* 15 U.S.C. § 1693*o*(a).

[24] As mentioned earlier, according to many stakeholders, the proposed legislation may result in remitters without proof of legal status requesting others with proof of legal status to make remittances on their behalf, therefore leaving the level of remittances potentially unchanged.

[25] Okla. Stat. Ann. tit. 63, § 2-503.1j.

[26] All the statements here are based on testimonial evidence. If there were other factors that affected remittances at the same time that the legislation was passed, it would have been difficult to isolate the effect of the legislation on remittances without proper analysis.

[27] *See* 31 C.F.R. § 1020.410(a) (recordkeeping requirements for banks); 31 C.F.R. § 1010.410(e) (recordkeping requirements for nondepository financial institutions).

[28] *See* 31 C.F.R. § 1020.220(a)(2).

[29] Profit margins represent the ratio of profits to sales revenue.

[30] National Research Council, *Principles and Practices for a Federal Statistical Agency: Fifth Edition* (Washington, D.C.: The National Academies Press, 2013), 18. The National Academies of Sciences, Engineering, and Medicine are private, nonprofit institutions that provide expert advice to the federal government. The principal statistical agencies of the federal government use this volume to guide their strategic planning, daily operations, and interactions with stakeholders. BEA is a signatory to the *Statement of Commitment to Scientific Integrity by Principal Statistical Agencies*, accessed November. 24, 2015, (https://www.bea.gov/_pdf/scientific_integrity_statement_of_the_principal_statistical_agen cies.pdf), which identifies this NRC publication, among other documents, as the foundation for achieving and maintaining scientific integrity within and among the principal statistical agencies.

[31] Remittance data used by BEA are censored because for some households the value of reported remittances is only partially known. BEA also assigned all households within a given range of family income the same income leading to measurement errors to the extent that households within a given range of family income do not, in fact, have the same income. With these data limitations, the methodology adopted by BEA results in biased estimates for the remittance rates.

[32] The CPS is sponsored jointly by Census and the U.S. Bureau of Labor Statistics. It is a primary source of labor force statistics for the population of the United States. In August 2008, Census sponsored a supplement to the monthly CPS questionnaire. The CPS Migration Supplement contained a section on monetary transfers to collect data about the frequency and amount of money sent and received by households in the United States to and from friends and relatives living outside the United States.

[33] A multiplicative model used by BEA expressed the remittance rates as a function of the product of various variables that BEA expected to have an effect on the remittance rate. In standard regression models, the remittance rate would have been expressed instead as a sum of these variables. Also instead of estimating the model using standard regression techniques, BEA adopted an iterative approach, which estimated the effect of one set of variables while assuming others to be held fixed at 1. In the second and third round, the effect of another set of variables was estimated using the results of the prior rounds fixed, and so on until all the estimates converged and stopped changing.

[34] The previous model combined detailed data on immigrants from the ACS with remittance rates by demographic category to estimate total remittances. The demographic characteristics included the country of origin, the duration of stay in the United States, and the presence of the immigrants' own children in the U.S. household.

[35] The country tiers in BEA's previous model were based on wealth and distance from the Unites States. The low tier was comprised of wealthy countries like Canada, Germany, and the United Kingdom. The middle tier consisted of middle-income countries like Argentina, Poland, and Thailand. The highest tier consisted of low-income countries throughout the world, including Latin American countries like Haiti, Honduras, and Mexico. The new geographical tier allocation is based on three immigration rules: whether the country a) is oversubscribed for applications for legal permanent residence, b) has temporary protected status, and c) has a visa waiver program with the United States and one "birth country characteristic" based on the World Bank's scores for government effectiveness and regulatory quality.

[36] Rachel Soloveichik and Anne Flatness, "Modeling Personal Transfers from the United States" (paper prepared for the 32nd General Conference of the International Association for Research in Income and Wealth [IARIW], Boston, MA, August 2012). The IARIW conference is an international forum for research on the measurement of income and related problems of statistical methodology. BEA staff also presented their work at a large Federal Committee on Statistical Methodology (FCSM) conference. FCSM is an interagency committee dedicated to improving the quality of federal statistics.

[37] The Information Quality Act (IQA) is the commonly used name for Section 515 of the Treasury and General Government Appropriations Act for Fiscal Year 2001. Pub. L. No. 106-554, tit. V, § 515, 114 Stat. 2763, 2763A-153 (2000) (codified at 44 U.S.C. § 3516 note). IQA requires OMB to provide guidance to federal agencies for ensuring and maximizing the quality, objectivity, utility, and integrity of information (including statistical information) disseminated by federal agencies. In accordance with the act, OMB developed policy and procedural guidance to federal agencies. 67 Fed. Reg. 8452 (Feb. 22, 2002). Under OMB's IQA guidelines, information deemed to be influential is to be held to a higher standard of quality; specifically, if an agency is responsible for disseminating influential scientific, financial, or statistical information, agency guidelines shall include a high degree of transparency about data and methods to facilitate the reproducibility of such information by qualified third parties. OMB defines influential, as used in the phrase influential scientific, financial, or statistical information, as meaning that the agency can reasonably determine that dissemination of the information will have or does have a clear and substantial impact on important public policies or important private sector decisions.

[38] Bureau of Economic Analysis, internal document, "Best Practices for Approving and Incorporating Changes in Methodology or in Data Sources."

[39] The best practice is included in the BEA internal document, "Best Practices for Approving and Incorporating Changes in Methodology or in Data Sources," which presents 10 practices BEA staff should follow. The practices are: justify the change, explain and document the change, provide experimental estimates, check for reasonableness, assess the resources required to implement the change, assess the impact on table designs and suppression, identify the time period the change could and/or should cover, notify and/or consult with those, both inside and outside of BEA, who use or provide the data, obtain higher level approval, and follow best practices guidelines for implementation.

[40] BEA told us that in 2011 or 2012 they had a slight change in their "logic" that caused the series to increase by 2 percent. BEA wanted to avoid a break in the series and did not want to revise previous years, so BEA put in this number as an adjustment factor.

[41] The descriptions were contained in the appendix of a research paper BEA used at professional conferences to describe the changes made to the model. Soloveichik and Flatness, "Modeling Personal Transfers."

[42] BEA staff noted that some of the recreated regressions produced results that differed slightly from the results reported in the conference paper. BEA staff explained that the difference might be due to typographical errors in the conference paper or to differences in the original and recreated regressions.

[43] The MESC is made up of selected senior members of the division responsible for estimating remittances, the Balance of Payments Division, including its chief, who offers feedback to guide and refine the staff's work.

[44] Soloveichik and Flatness, "Modeling Personal Transfers."

[45] BEA officials said that the review process culminated with a briefing to BEA's executive staff but did not provide us with documentation of the review. Articles in the *Survey* present BEA's latest national, international, regional, and industry estimates; describe the methodologies used to prepare the estimates; provide information about major revisions; discuss ongoing innovations; and generally keep users up to date on relevant BEA issues and initiatives.

[46] National Research Council, *Principles and Practices for a Federal Statistical Agency, 18.*

[47] BEA, internal document, "Best Practices Standards: BEA Data Handling and Documentation Standards." Outliers are extreme observations or observations that do not follow the pattern in the data and usually have an undue influence on the results in a regression model.

[48] BEA mentions in its paper that most of the households remit little or nothing while a few households give very large amounts and account for a significant fraction of total remittances. BEA staff stated that mean remittances drop by 60 percent if 175 households (out of more than 6,000) that remit $5000 or more are excluded. We do not know if and how BEA dealt with this issue. Moreover, we found that there were 51 households that were reported to have sent a remittance of $27,199. BEA staff told us that this was because the CPS top-codes the remittance variable so that any remittance value above $10,000 is coded as $27,199 as this is the mean of all remittances above $10,000. These instances, which are outliers in the data, significantly influence the resulting remittance rates but BEA could not provide documentation to show how influential these outliers actually are.

[49] BEA estimates remittances by using individual-level data from the ACS, but its estimation model is based on household data on remittances from the CPS. This poses a problem because CPS data reports remittances for the household as a whole and individual demographic characteristics as reported in the ACS can vary among individuals comprising a household.

[50] For example, in CPS data, *family income* is only reported as being within a range (e.g., $40,000 to $49,999). BEA assigns to all households with family income in the $40,000 to $49,999 range, the same family income of $45,000.

[51] BEA staff also told us that for the work on remittances, a top BEA economist provided direct supervisory suggestions on modeling and econometric approaches. Staff added that the work was subject to normal examination by the reviewers in the supervisory chain. However, BEA could not provide documentation of reviews in the supervisory chain, other than the MESC meeting minutes, in response to our request. Staff added that because the results were presented in two research forums, both the results and the underlying estimation approach and programming were scrutinized by other interested researchers. The extent of any peer review the paper received at the conferences is unclear because the audience feedback was not documented.

[52] As mentioned earlier, the guide for compilers provides recommendations designed to improve the quality of remittance data.

[53] International Monetary Fund, *International transactions in remittances: guide for compilers and users*. This publication provides guidelines for countries to improve the quality of remittance statistics by using suitable methodologies based on data availability and national circumstances. Variables can be converted in different forms such as quadratic or logarithmic to see if that better describes the relationship between dependent and independent variables.

[54] Goodness-of-fit indicators also allow for comparison between models as they give an indication of which model is better at representing the data.

[55] The R^2 test is a measure of the how well the proposed model fits the data. R^2 is most commonly expressed as a percentage ranging from 0 to 100. A low R^2 suggests that the model is a poor fit, while a high R^2 indicates that the model very closely matches the data. BEA's model produced an R^2 of 6.75 percent. BEA mentions an R^2 of 7.93 percent in the paper. But, according to the notes in one of the files we received from BEA, the analyst mentions that the number reported in the paper is inaccurate due to miscoding of one of the variables and the correct number is 6.75 percent. In other instances, BEA has reported an R^2 of 15.8 percent. BEA got this number when it ran the model again for us using a different dependent variable.

[56] The standard error is an estimate of the standard deviation of the coefficient and can be thought of as a measure of the precision with which the regression coefficient is measured. The standard error of the estimate thus can be thought of as a measure of the accuracy of predictions.

[57] Immigrants from a group of countries that remit the most compared to other immigrants are said to belong to the highest country tier.

[58] Statistical Policy Directive No. 1: Fundamental Responsibilities of Federal Statistical Agencies and Recognized Statistical Units, 79 Fed. Reg. 71,610 (Dec. 2, 2014).

[59] Similarly, BEA reports that individuals in households with 'MSA & Has roommates,' who remit to low-tier countries, and who have spent over 15 years in the United States remit 4.6 percent of their income. However, there are no such individuals in the BEA data. In fact, 25 percent of categories in which BEA classifies individuals are populated by five or fewer individuals. Hence, 25 percent of the estimated remittance rates as a fraction of income that BEA reports are based upon very little to no data on the individuals who are attributed these remittance rates by BEA.

[60] Statistical Policy Directive No. 4: Release and Dissemination of Statistical Products Produced by Federal Statistical Agencies, 73 Fed. Reg. 12,622 (Mar. 7, 2008).

[61] BEA estimates its model using a series of Ordinary Least Squares (OLS) regressions. When the dependent variable (remittances in BEA's model) is limited in some way, OLS estimates are biased.

[62] National Research Council, *Principles and Practices for a Federal Statistical Agency, 18.*

[63] In households that include both U.S.-born and foreign-born individuals, 50 percent of individuals in a household are U.S.-born, on average, and they account for 46 percent of the household's income on average.

[64] BEA officials told us that the extent to which various operating procedures are used depends on the procedure in question, the complexity and importance of the model or estimates, and the expertise of the staff assigned to their preparation.

[65] The number BEA uses is 2.76.

[66] G. Patricia de la Cruz, Luke J. Larsen, and Elizabeth M. Grieco, *An Overview of the August 2008 CPS Migration Supplement*, Working Paper No. 95, U.S. Census Bureau, May 2012.

[67] GAO-06-210.

[68] As mentioned previously, OMB's IQA guidelines define "influential" as meaning that an agency can reasonably determine that dissemination of the information will have or does have a clear and substantial impact on important public policies or important private sector decisions. 67 Fed. Reg. 8452, 8460. According to the guidelines, "integrity" refers to the security of information—the protection of the information from unauthorized access or revision, to ensure that the information is not compromised through corruption or falsification. 67 Fed. Reg. at 8460.

[69] U.S. Bureau of Economic Analysis, *Information Quality Guidelines* (Washington, D.C.: Updated September 2014), accessed July 6, 2015, http://www.bea.gov/about/infoqual.htm.

[70] The current account consists of transactions between U.S. residents and nonresidents in goods, services, primary income, and secondary income (including personal remittances).

[71] OMB guidelines allow agencies to weigh the costs (for example, costs attributable to agency processing efforts, respondent burden, maintenance of needed privacy, and assurances of suitable confidentiality) and the benefits of higher information quality in the development of information, and the level of quality to which the information disseminated will be held.

[72] OMB guidelines state that it designed the guidelines so that agencies will meet basic information quality standards. OMB adds that agencies shall adopt a basic standard of quality (including objectivity, utility, and integrity) as a performance goal and should take appropriate steps to incorporate information quality criteria into agency information dissemination practices.

[73] GAO, *Standards for Internal Control in the Federal Government*, GAO/AIMD-00-21.3.1 (Washington, D.C.: November 1999).

In: International Remittances
Editor: Cameron Slaton
ISBN: 978-1-53610-158-4

Chapter 3

INTERNATIONAL REMITTANCES: MONEY LAUNDERING RISKS AND VIEWS ON ENHANCED CUSTOMER VERIFICATION AND RECORDKEEPING REQUIREMENTS*

United States Government Accountability Office

WHY GAO DID THIS STUDY

The World Bank has estimated remittance outflows will reach $586 billion in 2015. However, some reports have indicated that remittance providers may be vulnerable to money laundering. Remittance providers are generally subject to both federal and state oversight.

GAO was asked to examine the potential illicit uses of remittances and assess whether requiring remittance senders to provide certain types of identification at a threshold below the current $3,000 level would be useful for U.S. AML efforts. This report examines (1) BSA remittance requirements that exist for remittance providers and related challenges that remittance providers face in complying with these requirements; (2) money laundering risks that remittances pose; and (3) stakeholders' views on the extent to which requiring remittance providers to verify identification and collect information at a lower dollar transaction amount than is currently required, or adding a requirement to

* This is an edited, reformatted and augmented version of a United States Government Accountability Office, Publication No. GAO-16-65, dated January 2016.

verify legal immigration status, would assist federal agencies' AML efforts. GAO reviewed laws and regulations, analyzed compliance data, and interviewed stakeholders (Financial Crimes Enforcement Network, regulators, remittance providers, law enforcement, and industry and other associations). GAO also interviewed a nongeneralizable selection of five money transmitters and four depository institutions based on factors such as remittance volume.

GAO is not making recommendations in this report. Agencies provided technical comments, which we incorporated as appropriate.

WHAT GAO FOUND

Financial institutions, such as money transmitters and depository institutions that provide remittance transfers—funds sent from individuals in one country to a recipient in another country—are subject to anti-money laundering (AML) requirements under the Bank Secrecy Act (BSA). For example, these remittance providers must report suspicious and other transactions, and obtain and record information for each funds transfer of $3,000 or more. Remittance providers GAO spoke with identified challenges related to BSA compliance—including monitoring large amounts of remittance data to identify and prevent illicit activity, and keeping up to date with the changing behavior of criminals. Further, some banks have ended account relationships with money transmitters—which need bank accounts to conduct business. Money transmitters going out of business could lead remittance senders to use informal methods that are less detectable.

Remittances can pose money laundering risks, as funds related to illicit activity may go undetected due to the large volume of transactions or remittance providers' inadequate oversight of the various entities involved. Stakeholders identified money laundering risks associated with customers, geographic location, products, and agents (entities authorized to provide remittances) that may fail to follow BSA requirements. Remittances can be used to launder proceeds from different types of criminal activities, including drug trafficking and human smuggling, through methods such as structuring. For example, a sender may structure remittances by breaking up a transaction into multiple transactions to avoid the $3,000 funds transfer threshold.

Many stakeholders said that a lower dollar threshold would benefit agencies' AML efforts, but verifying remitters' legal immigration status might not benefit such efforts. Law enforcement officials GAO spoke with said that a centralized database of remittances—one potential result of a proposed rule that would require remittance providers to report certain remittances data at a low dollar threshold—would be useful in assisting AML efforts. Larger remittance providers generally did not object to lowering the funds transfer threshold because they had already self-imposed lower thresholds. But bank regulators and some stakeholders said that a lower threshold could create additional recordkeeping requirements and costs for smaller providers and for customers. Stakeholders generally expressed concern that a requirement to check the legal status of a remittance sender might not assist AML efforts because it could lead senders to use less detectable forms of transmitting money.

ABBREVIATIONS

ACH	automated clearing house
AML	anti-money laundering
BSA	Bank Secrecy Act
CFPB	Consumer Financial Protection Bureau
DHS	Department of Homeland Security
DOJ	Department of Justice
FDIC	Federal Deposit Insurance Corporation
Federal Reserve	Board of Governors of the Federal Reserve
FFIEC	Federal Financial Institutions Examination Council
FinCEN	Financial Crimes Enforcement Network
FTC	Federal Trade Commission
IRS	Internal Revenue Service
NCUA	National Credit Union Administration
OCC	Office of the Comptroller of the Currency
Treasury	Department of the Treasury
USPS	United States Postal Service

* * *

January 15, 2016

The Honorable David Vitter
United States Senate

The Honorable Tom Price
Chairman
Committee on the Budget
House of Representatives

The World Bank has estimated global remittances for 2015 to be $586 billion with expected growth of 4.1 percent in 2016.[1] These remittance transfers—funds sent from individuals in one country to a recipient in another country—have gained attention over the years, largely because they are an important source of funds for some countries.[2] For many of the receiving countries, remittances are the largest source of foreign currency, often amounting to more than official foreign assistance from governmental international aid organizations and developed countries such as the United States. These transfers are generally considered a stable source of funds for receiving countries. Both nondepository and depository financial institutions provide money transfer services. Nondepository institutions providing such services are generally known as money transmitters. Depository financial institutions—such as banks and credit unions—also provide remittance transfer services. However, some international and U.S. agency reports have indicated that remittance providers may be vulnerable to money laundering and other illicit activities. For example, the Financial Action Task Force—an intergovernmental body developing and promoting policies to combat money laundering and terrorist financing—has identified instances in which entities providing remittance services, like other financial institutions, may have unintentionally or intentionally participated in money laundering.[3]

The United States has taken steps to regulate remittance providers and prevent money laundering. The Bank Secrecy Act (BSA) is an important tool in federal law enforcement efforts to detect and deter the use of financial institutions (including those that send remittances) for criminal activity, including money laundering and terrorist financing.[4] The Financial Crimes Enforcement Network (FinCEN), a bureau within the Department of the Treasury (Treasury), is responsible for administering the BSA. The BSA and implementing regulations generally require depository and other financial institutions—including money transmitters—to collect and retain various records of customer transactions, verify customers' identities in certain situations, maintain anti-money laundering (AML) programs, and report suspicious and other transactions. For example, financial institutions that provide money transfer services must obtain and retain specific information, such as name and address of the sender, for each transfer of $3,000 or more.[5]

For purposes of this report, we refer to the funding level at which requirements are imposed for obtaining identification and other information on remittances as the funds transfer threshold. FinCEN has published an advance notice of proposed rulemaking and a proposed rule related to the funds transfer threshold amount and related identification requirements.[6] Legislation has also been proposed that, if enacted, could affect identification requirements by requiring financial institutions that provide remittance services to request certain identification for remittance transfers at nearly any dollar amount. For example, the Remittance Status Verification Act would require remittance transfer providers to verify the legal status under the U.S. immigration laws of remittance senders and impose a fine on those who are unable to provide proof of their immigration status.[7]

You asked us to examine potential illicit uses of remittance transfers and determine, to the extent possible, whether information that would be collected under the proposed Remittance Status Verification Act would assist federal agencies' AML efforts. This report examines (1) BSA remittance requirements that exist for remittance providers and related challenges that remittance providers face in complying with these requirements; (2) the money laundering risks that remittance transfer methods pose; (3) stakeholders' views on the extent to which requiring money transmitters and depository institutions to verify identification and collect information at a lower dollar transaction amount than is currently required, or adding a requirement to verify legal immigration status, would assist federal agencies' AML efforts.[8]

To examine BSA remittance requirements that exist for remittance providers, we reviewed relevant laws and regulations. We obtained information from providers on their efforts to comply with BSA remittance requirements and the challenges they faced in doing so. We also obtained and analyzed available data on money transmitters' compliance with BSA-related requirements. We assessed the reliability of data by reviewing related documentation of the database from which the data come and also through interviews with agency officials, and found the data to be reliable for purposes of this report. To examine the money laundering risks posed by remittance transfers, we reviewed and summarized reports and documents that federal law enforcement, regulatory agencies, international organizations, and remittance providers maintain on money laundering through remittance transfers. To examine stakeholders' views on the extent to which lowering the funds transfer threshold for complying with recordkeeping requirements or adding a legal immigration status verification requirement would assist agencies' AML efforts, we reviewed an advance notice of proposed rulemaking, a proposed rule, and proposed legislation related to remittance transfers— including public comment letters available on the advance notice. For all objectives, we interviewed officials from FinCEN, federal law enforcement entities, federal and state regulators, industry associations, money transmitters, depository institutions, and policy and consumer advocacy groups. We judgmentally selected a cross-section of money transmitters and depository institutions that included five nondepository money transmitters and four depository institutions based on a number of factors, including the volume of remittances and diversity of countries serviced. Appendix I describes our objectives, scope, and methodology in greater detail.

We conducted this performance audit from October 2014 to December 2015 in accordance with generally accepted government auditing standards. Those standards require that we plan and perform the audit to obtain sufficient, appropriate evidence to provide a reasonable basis for our findings and conclusions based on our audit objectives. We believe that the evidence obtained provides a reasonable basis for our findings and conclusions based on our audit objectives.

BACKGROUND

Remittance Transfer Methods

Remittance transfers include many types of international transfers including cash-to-cash money transfers, international wire transfers, some prepaid card transfers, and automated clearing house (ACH) transactions.[9] According to a Treasury report on money laundering risks, 90 percent of households in the United States have an account with a depository institution such as a bank, thrift, or credit union.[10] Regardless, many people, particularly immigrants, use money services businesses to send money abroad because of convenience, cost, familiarity, or tradition. Money services businesses, which do not include depository institutions, are persons doing business in one or more of the following capacities, subject to exceptions:[11]

- Dealer in foreign exchange
- Check casher
- Issuer or seller of traveler's checks or money orders
- Provider or seller of prepaid access

- Money transmitter[12]
- United States Postal Service (USPS)[13]

There were about 29,000 registered money services businesses in the United States as of September 2015.[14] They typically work through agents—separate business entities generally authorized to, among other things, send and receive money transfers.[15] According to FinCEN 2011 survey data, the most frequent activity agents conducted was money transmitter services—transferring funds from one person to another person or location.

Remittances can be sent through, among others, money transmitters and depository institutions. Historically, consumers have primarily chosen to send remittances through money transmitters. Most remittance transfers are initiated in person at retail outlets that offer these services. Money transmitters generally operate through their own retail store fronts, or through grocery stores, financial services outlets, convenience stores, and other retailers that serve as agents. Depository institutions generally conduct remittances through their local branches. In one type of common money transmitter transaction—known as a cash-to-cash transfer (see fig. 1)—a sender can walk into a money transmitter agent location and provide cash to cover the transfer amounts and fees, and senders generally must provide basic information about themselves and the recipient (typically a name, address, and phone number) at the time of the transfer request. The agent processes the transaction, and the money transmitter's headquarters screens it for BSA compliance. The money can then be transferred to a recipient, usually through a distributor agent in the destination country. The money can be wired through the money transmitter's bank to the distributor agent's bank, or transferred by other means to a specified agent in the recipient's country. The distributor agent pays out cash to the recipient in either U.S. dollars or local currency.[16]

Figure 2 shows a bank-to-bank remittance transfer. The sender requests that money be removed from a bank account and transferred directly to the recipient's bank account. Figure 2 is an example of a simple funds transfer between two customers with only the remittance sender's and remittance recipient's banks involved. As the number of institutions involved increases, the transfer scenarios get more complicated. These more complicated scenarios are more common in the context of remittances, particularly if an originator's institution does not have a branch in the recipient's foreign location. In this case, one financial institution may rely upon established business relationships with additional financial institutions to complete the transaction—known as a correspondent banking relationship.[17]

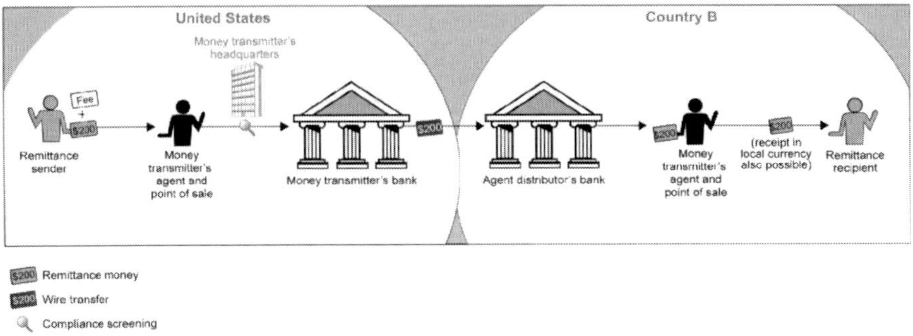

Source: GAO (analysis); Art Explosion (images). | GAO-16-65.

Note: Money transmitters often instruct agents to pay out funds to recipients before the funds are sent to the foreign location.

Figure 1. Example of a Money Transmitter Cash-to-Cash Remittance Transfer.

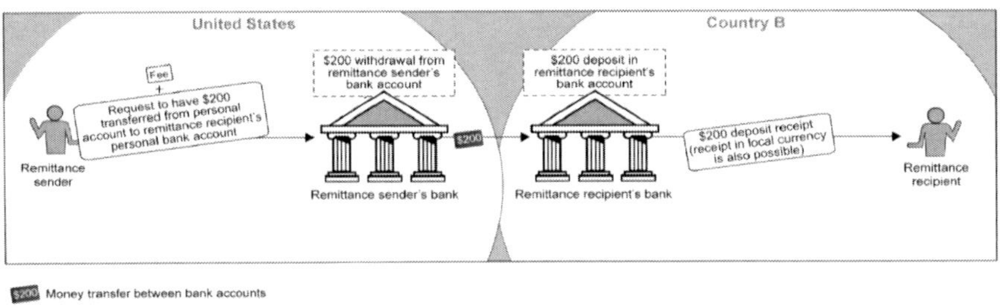

Source: GAO (analysis); Art Explosion (images). | GAO-16-65.

Note: This is an example of a simple funds transfer. More complicated transfers may involve more entities, such as correspondent banks.

Figure 2. Example of a Bank-to-Bank Remittance Transfer.

According to a 2011 report on remittance transfers from the Consumer Financial Protection Bureau (CFPB), industry participants and researchers report that cash-to-cash transfers made through money transmitters continue to account for the majority of personal transfers, rather than transfers through debits from or direct deposits to accounts held at depository institutions or credit unions.[18] Using state licensing data, CFPB estimated that money transmitters sent from the United States about 150 million international money transfers in 2012, with an estimated $49 billion total market value.[19] In contrast, according to reported depository institution data, depository institutions sent about 13 million international money transfers in calendar year 2014.[20] Although CFPB estimates show that money transmitters are responsible for sending the great majority of the remittance transfers, CFPB believes that the typical size of transfers sent by depository institutions is generally larger than the typical size of transfers sent by a money transmitter. A typical transfer sent by a depository institution may be in the thousands of dollars, while CFPB estimates that the typical size of remittance transfers sent by money transmitters is in the hundreds of dollars.[21] CFPB estimates from 2012 state supervisory data showed that the average transaction size for money transmitter remittances originating in the United States was about $300.[22]

As consumers and money transmitters become more technologically sophisticated, money transmitters have started offering an increasing range of other transfer methods. For example, according to the 2011 CFPB report on remittance transfers, several money transmitters have begun to permit consumers to transfer or receive money through accounts tied to e-mail addresses or mobile phone numbers (often called Internet or mobile phone "wallets"). According to a 2015 World Bank news release, despite its potential to lower costs, the use of mobile technology in cross-border transactions remains limited.[23]

Other Methods of Remittance Transfers

Remittance senders use a variety of other methods and products to send funds, such as prepaid cards sent by USPS; or the physical movement of money outside of the United States—such as using courier services that carry funds across the border.[24] One other method includes international money orders sent through USPS. Remittance senders can mail international money orders to about 30 countries through USPS's international mail services. Recipients can then cash these money orders either at local post offices or banks in destination countries.

Other methods for facilitating remittances include informal value transfer systems. Informal value transfer systems are often used in places where formal financial transactions are unavailable, expensive, or unreliable. A common type of informal value transfer is a hawala. The components of hawala that distinguish it from other remittance systems are trust and the extensive use of connections such as family relationships or regional affiliations.[25] Under the hawala system, a customer hands cash to a person known as a "hawaladar" and requests that an equivalent amount be delivered in local currency to a recipient in a different country. The hawaladar then contacts a hawaladar in the receiving country and asks that the funds be disbursed to the recipient. In most cases, fees are factored into the exchange rate or the amount that is disbursed.

Money Laundering

Money laundering—the process of making illegally gained proceeds appear legal—occurs in three distinct phases, as illustrated in figure 3. According to Treasury, placement occurs when illicitly obtained funds are introduced into the financial system. The funds are then separated from their criminal origins as they pass through several financial transactions in a process called layering. The next phase, integration, occurs when the funds are mixed with legitimately obtained money or used to acquire assets.

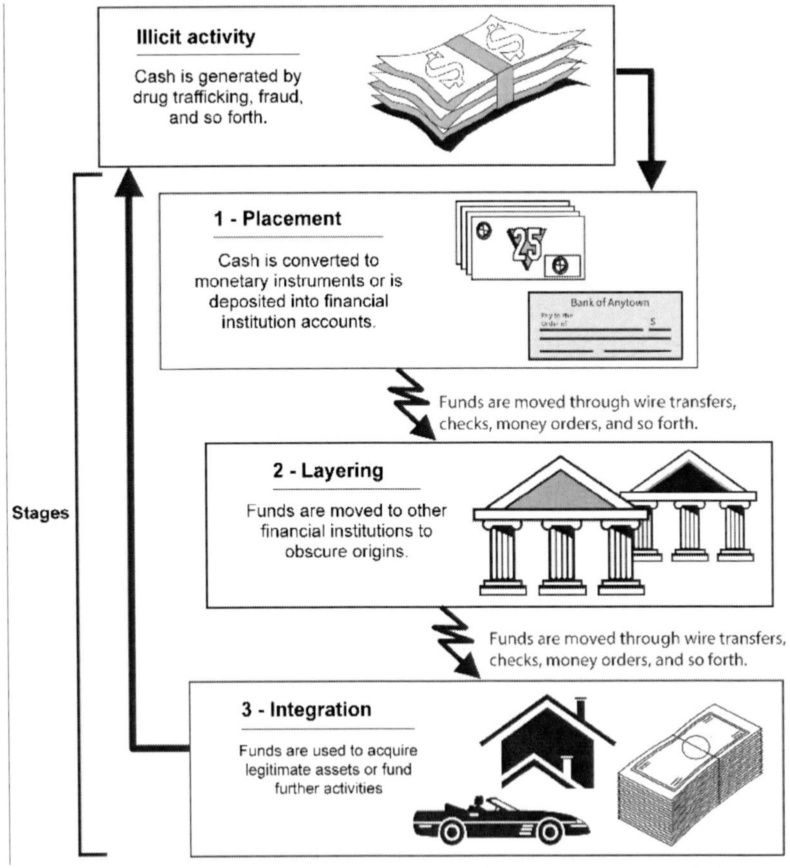

Source: Financial Crimes Enforcement Network, *FinCEN Related Series: An Assessment of Narcotics Related Money Laundering*, July 1992. | GAO-16-65.

Figure 3. Three Stages of Money Laundering.

Federal and State Oversight of Financial Institutions

Money transmitters and depository institutions are both generally subject to federal and state oversight. In general, money transmitters must register with FinCEN and provide information on structure and ownership.[26] Money transmitters also may be required to obtain licenses from states in which they are incorporated or conducting business. Depository institutions are regulated by state and federal banking regulators according to how they are chartered, and they provide related information when obtaining their charter.[27]

FinCEN often works in conjunction with federal and state regulators to support the examinations of both money transmitters and depository institutions. FinCEN issues regulations under the BSA and supports the examination functions performed by other federal regulators, including the federal banking regulators, the Internal Revenue Service (IRS), the Securities and Exchange Commission (SEC), and the Commodity Futures Trading Commission (CFTC).[28] FinCEN also collaborates with federal and state banking regulators and has issued joint guidance and rules with federal regulators. FinCEN relies on the federal banking regulators to examine depository institutions within their respective jurisdictions for BSA compliance. The federal banking regulators require institutions under their supervision to establish and maintain a BSA compliance program.[29] SEC has the authority to examine brokers and dealers in securities mutual funds for BSA compliance, while the CFTC has such authority with respect to futures commission merchants, introducing brokers in commodities.[30] The IRS has the authority to examine for BSA compliance financial institutions, such as money transmitters, that are subject to the BSA but are not currently examined by federal banking regulators for safety and soundness.[31]

To ensure consistency in the application of the BSA requirements, in 2008 FinCEN issued a BSA examination manual for use in reviewing money transmitters, including for IRS and state regulators. Similarly, in 2005 the federal banking regulators collaborated with FinCEN on a BSA examination manual that was issued by the Federal Financial Institutions Examination Council (FFIEC).[32] The manual is intended for federal bank examiners conducting BSA examinations of depository institutions. It was updated most recently in 2014 to further clarify supervisory expectations and regulatory changes.[33]

Depository institutions and money transmitters—in some states—are subject to safety and soundness examinations.[34] These on-site examinations are done periodically and assess an institution's adherence to laws and regulations such as the BSA, among other things. Federal banking regulators take a risk-based approach to BSA examinations— that is, they target key areas of risk or specific problems. In our prior work, we found that the risk-based approach allowed regulators to apply the appropriate scrutiny and devote resources to business lines or areas within institutions that pose the greatest risk for BSA noncompliance.[35]

FinCEN has overall authority for enforcement and compliance under the BSA, and may impose civil penalties and issue injunctions to compel compliance with BSA.[36] In addition, each of the federal banking regulators has the authority to initiate enforcement actions against supervised institutions for violations of law.[37] Federal banking regulators can also impose civil money penalties for BSA violations.[38] Under the BSA, IRS has certain authority that is delegated by FinCEN, and also has authority for investigating criminal violations.[39] The Department of Justice (DOJ) prosecutes violations of federal criminal money laundering statutes and violations of the BSA, and several law enforcement agencies can conduct BSA-related criminal investigations.

We did not identify any current federal requirement to verify the legal immigration status of a remittance sender. Federal legislation has been proposed that would require such verification. For example, the Remittance Status Verification Act of 2015, if enacted, would require each remittance transfer provider to request from each remittance transfer sender proof of the sender's legal status under U.S. immigration laws, and impose a fine on the sender—7 percent of the transfer amount—if the sender is unable to provide proof of legal immigration status.[40] One state has passed and others have proposed legislation related to verifying the legal immigration status of a sender. In July 2009, Oklahoma enacted a law requiring that a fee be imposed on all remittances that originate in Oklahoma, and customers are entitled to an income tax credit equal to the amount they paid when filing an individual income tax return in Oklahoma with either a valid Social Security or taxpayer identification number.[41] We also identified legislation that has been proposed—but not enacted—in several states between 2005 and October 2015 that would impose a fee on customers sending remittances who are unable to prove legal immigration status. For example, a bill that was introduced in Texas in March 2015 would require providers to charge a fee equal to 10 percent of a money transmission made by individuals unable to show proof of legal immigration status.[42]

BANK SECRECY ACT REQUIREMENTS AND COMPLIANCE-RELATED CHALLENGES

Money transmitters and depository institutions are subject to similar requirements under the BSA. They are generally required to design and implement a written AML program, report certain transactions to Treasury, and meet recordkeeping and identity documentation requirements for funds transfers of $3,000 or more. In our interviews, money transmitters and depository institutions indicated that they took steps to comply with these requirements, but identified some compliance-related challenges. These challenges included the cost of compliance, and derisking—the practice of depository institutions ending their relationships with money transmitters (who need bank accounts to conduct business) to avoid perceived regulatory concerns about facilitating money laundering.

Money Transmitters and Depository Institutions Are Subject to Similar BSA Requirements

AML Program Requirements

All financial institutions subject to the BSA—including money transmitters and depository institutions— are required to establish a written AML program.[43] At a minimum, each AML program must

- establish written AML compliance policies, procedures, and internal controls;
- designate an individual to coordinate and monitor day-to-day compliance;
- provide training for appropriate personnel; and
- provide for an independent audit function to test for compliance.[44]

FinCEN reported and the five money transmitters and four depository institutions we spoke with said that money transmitters and depository institutions had developed complex AML programs to meet FinCEN's requirements. Among the tools used were detailed software systems to help identify and monitor high-risk customers, and agent oversight and training.

- Money transmitters, depository institutions, and their respective industry associations told us they—or their members—used software systems that aided in their AML compliance, including what they described as robust monitoring programs that routinely evaluate high-risk customers. For example, one representative of a money transmitter we interviewed stated that the transmitter created a comprehensive member profile for each customer that identified their typical transactions. This system also automatically prevents the processing of transactions that seem abnormal based on a customer's profile. This representative indicated that they are developing a program that will provide a "risk score" for all customers as part of its efforts to conduct due diligence and monitor for suspicious activity.
- FinCEN has found that money transmitters have placed significant emphasis on AML program requirements including agent oversight, and consider compliance with BSA regulations part of their business models.[45] According to FinCEN, money transmitters try to mitigate agent risk by conducting due diligence on potential agents, making on-site visits to existing agents, reviewing and monitoring transactions, and engaging in mystery shopping—that is, unannounced testing of agents for money transmitters. A representative from a money transmitter industry association with whom we spoke said that money transmitters placed significant emphasis on agent training as a part of the steps they took to comply with AML program requirements.

IRS BSA examination data for fiscal years 2013 and 2014 showed that failure to comply with AML program requirements was the most frequently cited violation of money transmitters. See appendix II for more information.

Reporting Requirements

Depository institutions and money transmitters also must comply with certain reporting requirements. Money transmitters generally must file a suspicious activity report when a transaction involves or aggregates funds or other assets of at least $2,000 and they know, suspect, or have reason to suspect that the transaction is suspicious for one of several reasons.[46] Depository institutions are required to file a suspicious activity report when a transaction conducted by, at, or through the institution involves or aggregates at least $5,000 in funds or other assets and the institution knows, suspects, or has reason to suspect that the transaction is suspicious.[47]

According to a 2015 FinCEN report, suspicious activity reports play an integral role in law enforcement investigations and financial regulatory compliance at both the federal and state levels.[48] To ensure compliance, some money transmitters and depository institutions that we interviewed indicated that they filed suspicious activity reports on all suspicious transactions, regardless of size, and had designed programs to identify suspicious activity. A representative from another money transmitter told us that the institution did not file suspicious activity reports if it investigated a situation and found that there was a reasonable explanation for the transaction. However, the representative stated that the organization would file a suspicious activity report for a transaction of as little as $200 dollars if it suspected illicit activity. According to FinCEN, money transmitters have reportedly used social networking sites to verify identity during a suspicious activity report investigation, developed proprietary systems to identify suspicious activity, and placed accounts on hold after filing a suspicious activity report in order to ensure that they do not conduct further business with that customer.

A representative from another money transmitter described a series of software programs that it had developed and said that 95 percent of the overall suspicious activity that they identified was identified with the software. According to the representative, these systems check transactions monthly and look for illicit activity under the reporting threshold. The systems also aggregate different types of transactions to see if the same individual is transferring an amount of money above the reporting threshold through different products. Further, one industry group we interviewed that represents depository institutions indicated that institutions filed suspicious activity reports if they saw a series of transactions to high-risk corridors, such as Ukraine or the Middle East.

According to IRS BSA examination data for fiscal years 2013 and 2014, failure to file suspicious activity reports was the second most frequently cited violation during examinations of money transmitters. See appendix II for more information.

Recordkeeping and Identity Verification

Under the BSA, money transmitters and depository institutions are required to obtain and retain specified information, including the name and address of the sender, for all transfers in the amount of $3,000 or more, regardless of whether the sender is an established customer of the financial institution.[49] Recordkeeping and other BSA-related requirements for money transmitters and depository institutions include

- verifying customer identification (ID) when a transaction is conducted in person and the sender is not an established customer,
- recording certain specified customer and transaction information,
- providing certain information to the receiving money transmitter or other receiving financial institution,[50] and
- maintaining the record for 5 years from the date of transaction.

For transfers in the amount of $3,000 or more made by senders other than established customers, in person or not, money transmitters and depository institutions are required to obtain and retain a record of the name and address of the person placing the payment order, as well as the person's taxpayer identification number (Social Security number or employer identification number, for example).[51] If the person does not have a taxpayer identification number, the records must include an alien number, passport number and country of issuance, or notation in the record of the lack thereof.[52] For transfers made in person, money transmitters and depository institutions must, in addition to the items listed previously, also verify the identity of the person placing the order and obtain and retain a record of the type of identification reviewed as well as the number of the identification document. In verifying a sender's identity, institutions are required to examine a document—preferably with the person's name, address, and photograph—that is normally acceptable as a means of identification when cashing checks for persons other than established customers.

Depository institutions have some additional identification and verification requirements. As part of their BSA program requirements, depository institutions are required to implement a customer identification program appropriate for their size and type of business which, among other things, must include risk-based procedures for verifying the identity of each customer to the extent reasonable and practicable.[53] The customer identification program must contain procedures for opening an account that specify the identifying information that will be obtained from each customer, which shall include, at a minimum, name, date of birth, address, and identification number. The program must also include procedures for making and maintaining a record of a description of the methods used and the results of any measures undertaken to verify the identity of the customer, including a description of the resolution of any substantive discrepancy discovered when verifying the identifying information obtained.[54]

Some money transmitters and depository institutions that we spoke with said that they took steps beyond the minimum requirements to comply with the recordkeeping and identity verification requirements. All four depository institutions that we interviewed said that they imposed stricter requirements than minimally required to comply with the recordkeeping and identity verification requirements. Generally, these institutions limit remittance transfers to their customers only. Depository institutions must verify and record identification upon forming a customer relationship due to customer identification program requirements. Thus these depository institutions said that they generally verified identification for all remittance transfers when they established the customer relationship. One representative from a depository institution detailed the depository institution's policy for the collection of two levels of identification—primary and secondary identification. The official noted that the primary identification is aimed at complying with AML and customer identification program requirements, while the secondary identification is used for fraud prevention and can be as simple as a student identification card.

According to FinCEN, some money transmitters are reportedly implementing company standards that go beyond BSA requirements.[55] One representative from a money transmitter stated that the organization implemented a lower threshold of $750 for verifying identification. A representative from a money transmitter industry group explained it was common for money transmitters to impose thresholds lower than $3,000 for identity verification.

According to IRS BSA examination data for fiscal years 2013 and 2014, inadequate recordkeeping was the third most frequently cited BSA violation during examinations of money transmitters. See appendix II for more information.

Expectations for Depository Institutions That Have Money Transmitters as Customers

Depository institutions open and maintain accounts for money transmitters. FinCEN and the federal banking regulators have provided interagency guidance for depository institutions that provide banking services to money transmitters, which outlines the following minimum due diligence expectations based on BSA requirements:

- applying the depository institution's customer identification program;
- confirming FinCEN registration, if required;
- confirming compliance with state or local licensing requirements, if applicable;

- confirming agent status, if applicable;[56] and
- conducting a basic BSA risk assessment to determine the level of risk associated with the account and whether further due diligence is necessary.[57]

A representative from a depository institution whom we interviewed stated that the institution conducted due diligence on money transmitter customers that included an on-site visit and a review of their financial statements. This representative also explained that the institution inspected the AML program that the money transmitter had in place. According to the interagency guidance for depository institutions that provide banking services to money transmitters, regulators expect the depository institution to conduct a risk assessment of the account and confirm the money transmitter's compliance with applicable licensing and registration requirements. The guidance notes that regulators do not expect depository institutions to uniformly review the AML program of all money transmitters that are customers, but that a depository institution's level of review of a money transmitters' AML program should be based on the assessed risks of the particular relationship.

Money Transmitters and Depository Institutions Identified Challenges Related to BSA Compliance

Money transmitters, depository institutions, and industry associations we interviewed identified some challenges in complying with BSA requirements, including suspicious activity report confidentiality requirements, derisking, monitoring and examining remittance data, and costs.

Suspicious Activity Report Confidentiality Requirements

Officials we spoke with from a money transmitter and an industry association representing depository institutions stated that suspicious activity report confidentiality requirements hindered global money transmitters and depository institutions from meeting their AML risk management and monitoring requirements. The BSA prohibits financial institutions that file a suspicious activity report from notifying any person involved in the transaction that the transaction has been reported.[58] FinCEN has explained that unauthorized disclosure of suspicious activity reports could undermine investigations by tipping off suspects, deterring financial institutions from filing suspicious activity reports, and threatening the safety and security of institutions and individuals filing such reports. FinCEN warns that the disclosure of suspicious activity reports compromises the essential role they play in protecting the financial system and in preventing and detecting financial crimes and terrorist financing.

According to FinCEN and the federal banking regulatory guidance, BSA's confidentiality provision generally prohibits a depository institution from disclosing or revealing a suspicious activity report.[59] FinCEN and the federal banking regulators have amended suspicious activity report confidentiality rules and provided guidance to clarify the confidentiality requirements for depository institutions. The 2006 guidance states that a U.S. branch or agency of a foreign depository institution may share a suspicious activity report with its head office outside the United States. In addition, it states that a U.S. depository institution may disclose a suspicious activity report to its controlling company, no matter where it is located. The depository institution must have written confidentiality agreements or arrangements in place specifying that the head office or controlling company must protect the confidentiality of suspicious activity reports through appropriate internal controls. In 2010, FinCEN issued further guidance stating that a depository institution may share a suspicious activity report or any information that would reveal the existence of such a report with domestic affiliates subject to a suspicious activity report regulation, but cannot share suspicious activity reports with foreign branches of U.S. banks.[60] In December 2010, FinCEN amended its BSA regulations on the confidentiality of suspicious activity reports to state that the confidentiality requirements do not prohibit the disclosure of the underlying facts, transactions, and documents upon which a suspicious activity report is based.[61] The preamble to the final rule clarifies that confidentiality rules do not apply to information shared with entities in the ordinary course of business that identify suspicious content but do not indicate whether the information was filed in a suspicious activity report.[62] One industry association requested further guidance—in addition to the language in FinCEN's 2010 final rule clarifying confidentiality rules—on what information could be shared when depository institutions provided information to foreign banks, but could not reveal the existence of a suspicious activity report.

Derisking

With respect to money transmitters, derisking—the practice of depository institutions limiting certain services or ending their relationships with entities to, among other things, avoid perceived regulatory concerns about facilitating money laundering—poses challenges for depository institutions and money transmitters.[63] Depository institutions face compliance challenges in managing risk appropriately while avoiding indiscriminately terminating or refusing to open accounts for money transmitters. Money transmitters need bank accounts to conduct business, including settling accounts among agents and other financial institutions. In 2014, FinCEN reported that some money transmitters are losing access to banking services with depository institutions due to derisking.[64] Additionally, three representatives from money transmitters and affiliated industry groups we spoke with described difficulties in maintaining and forming relationships with depository institutions. A representative from a money transmitter industry group told us that depository institutions should be able to rely on the fact that money transmitters are subject to BSA requirements and examinations by state and federal regulators.

According to the FFIEC BSA/AML Examination Manual, however, a number of characteristics of money transmitters could expose depository institutions to risk.[65] For example, the manual specifies that, among other things, money transmitters lack ongoing customer relationships and require minimal or no identification from customers, engage in frequent currency transactions, and are subject to varying levels of regulatory requirements and oversight. Nearly all representatives from depository institutions and affiliated industry groups whom we interviewed said that they had difficulty doing business with money transmitters because of the increased regulatory risk. For example, representatives from all three depository institutions' industry associations added that it was sometimes easier to sever relationships with money transmitters than face the possibility of compliance failure.

Some federal banking regulators have acknowledged that some depository institutions have limited certain types of banking services because of concerns that money transmitter customers might not comply with the BSA. However, federal banking regulators and FinCEN encourage depository institutions to practice a risk-based approach when evaluating individual customers. According to FinCEN's public statement issued in 2014, money transmitters play an important role in the financial services sector.[66] Derisking related to money transmitters could reduce BSA reporting in the financial system if the transmitters went out of business and more remittance transfers were sent via informal methods, which are often outside the reporting system. FinCEN's 2014 public statement discouraged derisking and emphasized that institutions were expected to properly manage and mitigate any risks that money transmitters presented on a case-by-case basis. FDIC has provided similar guidance, and the Comptroller of the Currency has publicly echoed it by explaining that high-risk customers should be managed with strong risk management and controls rather than with a strategy of total avoidance.[67] According to a Treasury official, bank regulators have taken very few public enforcement actions against depository institutions for deficiencies related to the money transmitters who have accounts with them.

In a 2015 global Anti-Money Laundering Survey of AML specialists, the Association of Certified Anti-Money Laundering Specialists found that more than one-third of respondents reported that the institutions they worked for had exited lines or segments of business in the past 12 months due to perceived regulatory risk.[68] While this information was not specific to derisking and money transmitters, it speaks to the idea of depository institutions managing regulatory risk by exiting business lines that they perceive to be too risky. Furthermore, two World Bank surveys conducted in 2015, and the corresponding reports, found that some depository institutions are reducing access to financial services for remittance providers in some countries and regions.[69] One of these reports was on a survey of derisking, for which they use the Financial Action Task Force definition of the term—the phenomenon of financial institutions terminating or restricting business relationships with clients or categories of clients to avoid, rather than manage, risk. According to the report, the survey indicates that derisking exists in some countries. The main drivers cited for account closures of money transmitters mainly included: profitability, pressure from other entities involved—such as correspondent banks, fear of regulatory scrutiny, lack of confidence in money transmitters' procedures, and reputational risk. The reports make recommendations, including for governments to monitor correspondent banking and money transmitters' access to financial services, and to have legal and regulatory AML frameworks in place and ensure that financial institutions are being effectively supervised for compliance with these standards—including ensuring and communicating risk-based supervision and enforcement. The recommendations also suggest that money transmitters should improve their AML controls to reduce their risk profile, and national authorities and financial institutions need to improve and communicate their overall understanding of risk.

Challenges in Monitoring and Examining Remittance Data

Money transmitters and depository institutions that we interviewed indicated that they faced challenges in monitoring and examining data from remittance transactions. Representatives from three of the four depository institutions we spoke with described difficulties they faced in identifying and preventing illicit activity, including the need to constantly monitor and examine transactions and identify structuring activity. FinCEN similarly recently reported that one of the key challenges banks faced was adequately adapting their controls on a timely basis to eliminate vulnerabilities that criminals were exploiting. One money transmitter industry group representative told us that keeping money transmitters' monitoring systems up to date with the changing behavior of criminals was a challenge. This representative said that law enforcement and FinCEN are helpful in providing them with guidance and information on new patterns of activity. For example, FinCEN issued a notice in 2014 to be aware of illicit movement of money from the Los Angeles garment district to Mexico and Colombia on behalf of prominent drug trafficking organizations. In the 2015 Association of Certified Anti-Money Laundering Specialists survey, 38 percent of respondents cited insufficient/outdated technology as a compliance challenge that could serve as a possible barrier to the monitoring of remittance transactions.

Compliance Costs

Both money transmitters and depository institutions that we spoke with said that the costs of complying with BSA requirements and potential new rules presented a challenge. One money transmitter industry group representative told us that compliance cost is a challenge that is quite substantial for money transmitters. For example, one large money transmitter told us that they are implementing a system to better monitor their customers that is costing them millions of dollars. A representative from another money transmitter told us that there are costs associated with compliance, including additional expenses for training employees and integrating a system that helps the transmitter identify suspicious activity and prevent illicit transactions. Officials from a credit union we spoke with said that compliance cost is a challenge for smaller credit unions because establishing effective BSA and AML programs is expensive and smaller institutions have fewer resources to absorb such expenses. One industry association representing community banks added that it is especially difficult for smaller institutions that do not have the resources to spend time and money to monitor and examine riskier customers that require enhanced due diligence. Furthermore, a representative from a large depository institution said that it was becoming increasingly expensive to keep up with compliance costs as the regulatory environment seems to be getting stricter with a recent number of consent orders and fines.

Personal Liability of Compliance Officers

Money transmitters and depository institutions that we spoke with identified concerns about the personal liability of compliance officers. In January 2014, FinCEN's director acknowledged that there had been calls for more accountability in compliance failures, in particular for a focus on individuals as well as institutions.[70] The director stressed the importance of holding accountable those who violated BSA requirements. In 2014, FinCEN assessed a $1 million civil money penalty against the Chief Compliance Officer of a large money transmitter concluding that he willfully violated the BSA requirements to implement and maintain an effective AML program and to report suspicious activity.[71] FinCEN found that as a result of the Chief Compliance Officer's AML failures, agents and outlets—that the money transmitter's personnel knew or suspected were involved in fraud and money laundering—were allowed to continue to use the money transmitter's money transfer system.

Officials we spoke with from six institutions representing money transmitters and depository institutions expressed concern about the liability of compliance officers under the BSA, but one official representing a credit union thought personal responsibility was long overdue. One money transmitter said that holding compliance officers personally accountable was inappropriate. An industry association representative said that it was counterproductive if a compliance officer was negligent and not complicit in illegal activity and stated that hiring and retaining compliance officers was becoming a challenge. Another industry association representing depository institutions told us that if there is a trend of holding compliance officers responsible for AML failures, it may become increasingly difficult to hire qualified people for the position. Officials from one credit union and two industry associations stated that the personal liability of compliance officers could cause compliance officers to be more risk averse—potentially resulting in the decisions of depository institutions to derisk money transmitter accounts in order to avoid personal liability and scrutiny. However, an official from a credit union said that the shift toward compliance officer personal responsibility was probably long overdue. FinCEN and OCC issued statements and advisories promoting the culture of compliance and stating that an important aspect of a culture of compliance is leadership's responsibility for the performance, including the institution's compliance with BSA requirements.[72] DOJ has also issued a memo that stresses the importance of individual accountability to combat corporate fraud and other misconduct, and provides DOJ's policy for investigations of corporate misconduct that focuses on individual liability.[73]

Remittance Transfers Pose Money Laundering Risks

Remittance transfers are vulnerable to money laundering due to factors such as the large volume of transactions and the global reach of large remittance transfer companies. Stakeholders have identified money laundering risks of remittance transfers including risks involving agents, customers, geographic location, and products. Remittance transfers can be used to launder proceeds from different types of criminal activities, including drug trafficking, human smuggling, and consumer fraud.

Agents, Customers, Geographic Location, and Products Can Pose Money Laundering Risks

Agency officials, industry stakeholders (including money transmitters and depository institutions), and international organizations have identified several types of money laundering risks associated with remittance transfers, including risks involving agents, customers, geographic location, and products. Remittance transfers are vulnerable to money laundering due to factors such as the large volume of transactions, which can make it difficult to detect laundered funds, and the global reach of large remittance transfer companies, which can allow customers to move funds easily around the world. Furthermore, Treasury reported that deficient compliance with BSA requirements could leave money transmitters and depository institutions vulnerable to money laundering.[74] Additionally, FinCEN, law enforcement, and international organizations said that certain remittance transfer methods, such as unregistered informal value transfer systems discussed earlier, pose risks that are difficult to manage because law enforcement has limited visibility of these transactions. However, they cautioned that a single risk may not indicate money laundering, but risks should be considered in the aggregate.

Agent Risk

Money transmitters often work with a number of agents, and maintaining adequate oversight can be challenging, given the decentralized nature of the agent system. In a 2011 survey that FinCEN conducted, 170 money services businesses—often working in the capacity of a money transmitter—reported that they had over 230,000 agents—with 3 of these money services businesses reporting that they had over 20,000 agents each.[75] These agents present money laundering risks if they knowingly or unknowingly fail to follow BSA requirements or the policies and programs established by the money transmitter. For example, an agent may not follow the recordkeeping requirements for transfers above the regulatory funds transfer threshold or above lower thresholds that a remittance provider has self imposed.

Customer Risk

Customers are another source of risk, because in certain instances they may be able to launder money while remaining anonymous. For example, money launderers may use false identities or straw men (individuals hired to conduct transfers on behalf of others) in order to keep from being identified as the original source of the funds. Money launderers may also keep transactions below the regulatory recordkeeping and reporting requirements or the money transmitter's self-imposed recordkeeping requirements in order to remain anonymous. The FFIEC BSA/AML Examination Manual provides examples of suspicious customer activity that may indicate money laundering. These examples include identification documents that cannot be easily verified; the use of different taxpayer identification numbers with variations of the same name; frequent or large transactions with no record of past or present employment; and reluctance to provide identification for transactions subject to identification requirements. Law enforcement officials added other indicators, such as receiving multiple transfers from different geographic locations (both domestic and international), and using variations of names and addresses that are inconsistent with the identification provided.

Geographic Location Risk

Agency officials, industry stakeholders, and international organizations generally agreed that certain geographic locations may be more vulnerable to money laundering via remittances. For example, FinCEN has noted the importance of factoring in geographic risk for both depository institutions and money transmitters. In addition, one regulator said that international transfers were at a high risk for money laundering because, depending on the destination country, transparency could be lost if the country receiving the remittance did not have the same AML standards as the United States. The FFIEC BSA/AML Examination Manual states that financial institutions with foreign offices or branches should comply with local requirements and be consistent with the U.S. bank's standards; however, foreign offices' or branches' standards may need to be tailored for local laws and regulations. The FFIEC BSA/AML Examination Manual also states that depository institutions should factor geographic location into their BSA risk assessments. While geographic location alone does not determine a customer's or transaction's money laundering risk level, according to the FFIEC BSA examination manual, certain characteristics can contribute to a location's designation as high risk.[76] A number of sources exist for money transmitters and depository institutions to identify high-risk geographic locations. Some of these include countries subject to Office of Foreign Assets Control sanctions, jurisdictions determined to be of "primary money laundering concern" by Treasury, High Intensity Financial Crime Areas, and those identified by the Financial Action Task Force as having deficient AML and counterterrorist financial measures.[77]

Products/Services Risk

The U.S. financial system provides a wide range of products and services that help create a complex environment in which, according to Treasury, both legitimate and unlawful activity can take place. According to the FFIEC BSA/AML Examination Manual, certain products and services, such as funds transfers, may pose a higher risk of money laundering because of the degree of anonymity they can offer. For example, emerging technologies can offer a degree of anonymity and new providers entering the market may not be compliant with existing regulations. The Financial Action Task Force identified money laundering and terrorist financing risks associated with mobile payments because these services can sometimes allow for anonymous transactions depending on the level of AML measures the mobile payments provider has in place. The Financial Action Task Force also reported that virtual currency—digital representations of value that are not government-issued, such as Bitcoin—could facilitate international remittances as virtual currency-based products and services are developed. FinCEN recognizes money laundering vulnerabilities in virtual currencies. In 2013 FinCEN issued guidance clarifying that administrators and exchangers of virtual currency were considered money transmitters and thus were subject to the same BSA requirements.[78]

The FFIEC BSA/AML Examination Manual listed correspondent account relationships as services, in particular, for which depository institutions should manage risk. As discussed earlier, multiple depository institutions may be involved in remittance transfers—known as correspondent banking relationships—and assessing the risk of each of them can be difficult.

According to FinCEN, approximately 300 banks in the United States provide correspondent banking services to foreign financial institutions. U.S. banks may receive funds or instructions for a funds transfer from a foreign correspondent bank. While U.S. banks may have a relationship with the foreign bank, they probably do not have a relationship with the originator of the funds transfer. For this reason, the FFIEC BSA/AML Examination Manual and FinCEN stress the importance of conducting appropriate due diligence with foreign banks as part of risk management programs.

Remittances Have Been Used to Launder Proceeds from Criminal Activity

Federal agencies and international organizations have identified instances where remittances have been used to launder proceeds from illicit activities such as drug trafficking, human smuggling and trafficking, and consumer fraud. To transmit illicit funds, money launderers use underground providers such as couriers, hawaladars, and straw men (persons hired to conduct transfers for others), or transfers made by several people to the same beneficiary. They may also provide false information during the identification process for a remittance. Structuring is another means of disguising large proceeds from illicit activities. It generally involves dividing a large transaction into several smaller transactions to evade BSA reporting requirements.[79] As shown in figure 4, an individual could remit $1,000 to the same beneficiary in three separate transactions. Since each of the individual remittances is below the $3,000 reporting threshold, this activity avoids recordkeeping and reporting requirements. Structuring is considered both a criminal activity in itself and a potential method for hiding the proceeds of other suspicious activity.[80]

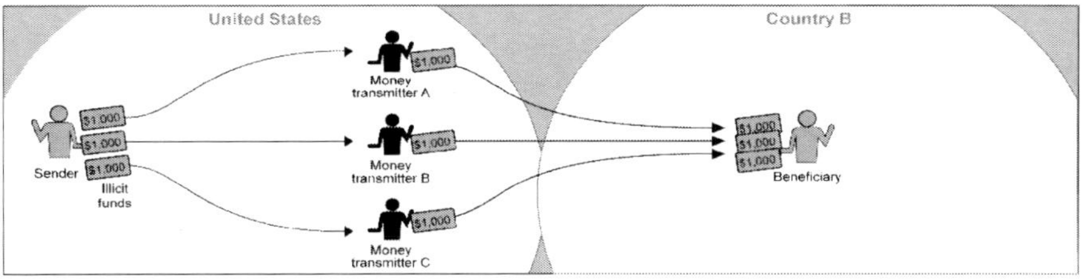

Source: GAO (analysis); Art Explosion (images). | GAO-16-65.

Figure 4. Example of Structuring to Launder Illicit Funds.

In its 2015 National Money Laundering Risk Assessment, Treasury identified structuring as a common money laundering method used in the United States, and a money laundering vulnerability for money transmitters.[81] FinCEN data on suspicious activity report filings related to international remittances by money services businesses, including money transmitters, showed that structuring—after fraud—was the second most frequently cited suspicious activity category in 2014.[82] Treasury has identified instances in which structuring was used to hide and transmit illicit funds, such as the following:

- In 2007, a task force made up of federal, state, and local law enforcement in New York and New Jersey conducted a sting operation in which 27 money transmitters were prosecuted for facilitating money laundering. The money transmitters allegedly agreed to transfer drug proceeds to Colombia and structured the transactions in order to avoid federal recordkeeping and reporting requirements.[83]
- In 2008, in California, four family members were indicted for running a small human smuggling ring that had allegedly been bringing illegal immigrants into the United States from Mexico since 1996, earning approximately $50,000 a year.[84] According to the indictment, the defendants instructed the sponsors of the illegal immigrants to pay the smuggling fee, which ranged from $1,000 and $3,000 per person, via nonbank wire transfer and to structure the payment across multiple wires.
- In a 2011 case, seven people were sentenced for money laundering and drug trafficking involving the transfer of drugs from the Virgin Islands to Alaska. Hundreds of thousands of dollars in payment for the drugs were sent using a large money transmitter to send wire transfers in amounts averaging less than $2,000 per wire.[85]

Drug Trafficking

Transactions made using cash generated from drug trafficking can be structured to remain below the recordkeeping and reporting thresholds. In 2010 a Florida bank was charged with willfully failing to establish an adequate AML program. The charge followed a criminal investigation into $13 million of wire transfers initiated by Mexican casas de cambio (exchange houses) from correspondent accounts at the bank to pay for aircraft subsequently used to transport illegal drugs to the United States.[86] In addition, officials at the

Department of Homeland Security (DHS) told us that employees of a money transmitter helped launder over $1 million in drug proceeds to the Dominican Republic.

Human Smuggling and Human Trafficking

Human smuggling involves bringing or attempting to bring undocumented immigrants into the United States.[87] Human trafficking involves the use of force, fraud or coercion to recruit, harbor, transport, provide, or obtain persons for purposes including forced labor and sexual exploitation.[88] There are a number of stages involved in human smuggling and in human trafficking during which smugglers and traffickers may need to interact with remittance providers. For example, to avoid detection, smugglers may make multiple remittance payments below the recordkeeping and reporting thresholds to people who are paid to move undocumented immigrants to the United States. In 2010 a large money transmitter entered into a $94 million settlement with the state of Arizona after it was accused of processing over $500 million in payments to human smugglers annually between 2003 and 2007.[89]

One money transmitter we spoke with provided internal guidance that it relies on to help identify possible human smuggling payments. This guidance included the following examples:

- A customer picks up money transfers in agent locations along the U.S. border from multiple senders in various parts of the United States. All of the transactions are for similar dollar amounts.
- A customer picks up a money transfer at an agent location along the U.S. border and is accompanied by another person. The other person appears to be telling the customer what to do. After the transaction is completed, the customer gives the money to the other person.

FinCEN has issued guidance to financial institutions listing red flags that could indicate human smuggling or trafficking.[90] The guidance encourages financial institutions to file a suspicious activity report if they suspect a transaction has no legitimate business purposes and could be related to human smuggling or trafficking.

This FinCEN guidance also states that no single transaction by itself is a clear indicator of human smuggling or human trafficking but that several warning signs can indicate this type of behavior. These include multiple wire transfers below the $3,000 threshold sent to a common beneficiary from various locations, wire transfers from countries with high migrant populations, and the existence of a potential funnel account.[91] The amounts wired may be kept below the reporting threshold and occur in locations where the customer does not reside. According to Treasury, efforts by state and federal law enforcement to curb the use of money transmitters to pay human smugglers along the southwest border has resulted in a shift to funnel accounts, using the banking system rather than money transmitter networks.

However, law enforcement officials from the southwest border High Intensity Financial Crime Area told us that, in their experience, a large percentage of human smuggling fees were sent using money transmitters because these providers offered a quick and reliable method of transfer with some degree of perceived anonymity for the smugglers and their couriers. These officials said that over $12 million in suspected illicit human smuggling proceeds were sent to Texas border cities through money transmitters in the 4-month period between January and April 2015.

Consumer Fraud

Money transmitters and depository institutions have been used to facilitate consumer fraud, such as lottery scams or scams involving a relative's stolen identity, as identified in a recent enforcement action, Federal Trade Commission (FTC) consumer complaint data, and by the Internet Crime Complaint Center—the federal cybercrime complaint organization. The Internet Crime Complaint Center describes various schemes that defraud consumers into wiring funds directly to fraudsters, resulting in virtually unrecoverable losses to the victim and with little recourse. One federal banking regulatory official explained that fraudsters request victims to use wire transfer services to send funds because the money moves fast and they can take the money before the victim discovers the scam.

In 2012, DOJ found that a large money transmitter's agents knowingly participated in a scheme in which U.S. customers wired funds to Canada in response to fraudulent claims that they were required to pay a fee or tax before receiving a lottery winning that they were falsely told was due them.[92] The large money transmitter agreed with DOJ to address the problems in its AML program that facilitated fraud. According to recent FTC consumer compliant data, the highest reported payment method used in cross-border fraud complaints in 2014 was a wire transfer.[93] This consumer complaint data showed that 55 percent of the complaints from U.S. consumers who paid companies located in Canada reported wire transfer as the payment method, and 78 percent of the complaints from U.S. consumers who paid other foreign companies reported that wire transfers were the payment methods. Treasury reported that, along with drug trafficking, fraud generates a large amount of illicit proceeds in the United States each year.[94] According to FinCEN data on suspicious activity report filings related to international remittances by money services businesses, including money transmitters, fraud was the most frequently cited suspicious activity in 2014.[95]

Many Stakeholders Supported Lowering the Funds Transfer Threshold, but Cited Concerns with Verifying Remitters' Legal Immigration Status

Many stakeholders, including law enforcement officials, four of the five money transmitters we spoke with, and all four depository institutions, told us they generally supported or were already using a funds transfer threshold lower than the existing $3,000 for obtaining identification and other information on remittances. For example, law enforcement officials said that a centralized database of remittance transfers—one result of a proposed rule that would require remittance providers to report certain remittance data at low dollar thresholds—would help identify illicit activity and be useful in assisting AML efforts. Most larger money transmitters and larger depository institutions we spoke with were already using thresholds below $3,000. However, some stakeholders said that a lower threshold could negatively affect small providers. For example, federal and state banking regulators said that a lower threshold would likely create additional recordkeeping requirements and costs for some providers and customers. But, stakeholders generally said that a requirement to check the legal immigration status of remittance senders would not significantly benefit AML efforts, noting that the requirement could lead senders to use less detectable forms of transmitting money.

Many Stakeholders Supported a Lower Threshold, but Some Were Concerned about Additional Recordkeeping Requirements and Costs

Law enforcement officials generally stated that a funds transfer threshold lower than the existing $3,000 threshold would benefit agencies' AML efforts. Several law enforcement agencies, including DHS, DOJ, and IRS, indicated in

2006 that additional information collected as a result of lowering or eliminating the threshold would prove beneficial to investigations including money laundering.[96] The law enforcement officials added at that time that lowering or eliminating the threshold could disrupt illicit transfers and make them more expensive for perpetrators. For example, DOJ law enforcement officials stated that a lower threshold would increase the cost of laundering money, because more transfers would have to be structured to stay below the threshold. DHS officials we spoke with recommended a $500 funds transfer threshold, which they said would be low enough to limit structuring capabilities but would not impede legitimate transactions. DOJ officials, while noting the benefits of a lower threshold, also identified some concerns. For example, DOJ's letter commenting on the 2006 advance notice of proposed rulemaking (2006 advance notice) stated that there were no specific data showing that a lower threshold would benefit law enforcement, as transactions structured at smaller values could approach the range of legitimate transactions and thus become more difficult to detect.[97]

Many law enforcement officials supported a requirement for reporting information on remittances. BSA requirements generally focus on recording funds transfers rather than reporting them, unless they constitute certain types of transactions such as suspicious transactions. Several law enforcement agencies supported and noted the benefits of adding such a reporting requirement in a 2006 FinCEN study.[98] Furthermore, DHS and DOJ officials we spoke with for this report said that information on remittance senders that could be collected in a centralized database could be analyzed to help identify illicit activity and would be useful in AML efforts. DHS officials noted that they used a comprehensive database to track remittances from 10 of the largest money transmitters that report remittance data along the southwest border to identify human smuggling networks. These officials said that having these type of data at the federal level would be useful. One DOJ official stated that the option most favorable to law enforcement in investigating illicit transfers would be FinCEN's 2010 proposed rule, Cross-Border Electronic Transmittals of Funds (2010 proposed rule), which would require depository institutions and money transmitters to report cross-border electronic transmittals at a zero dollar threshold and $1,000 threshold, respectively—lower dollar thresholds than providers are currently required to use.[99] The reporting requirement would provide a searchable database of remittances for law enforcement to analyze, while information provided by a lower funds transfer threshold without a reporting requirement would have to be requested by law enforcement on a case-by-case basis. FinCEN is still evaluating ways to implement the 2010 proposed rule in a way that takes into account industry concerns such as the cost to financial institutions and the government's ability to implement, manage, and support a reporting system. FinCEN also continues to consider the appropriate reporting thresholds.

Four of the five money transmitters we spoke with, and all four depository institutions, told us they generally supported or were already using a lower funds transfer threshold for obtaining identification and other information on remittances. Stakeholders we spoke with noted that these providers were generally already collecting and maintaining information at lower thresholds. Larger depository institutions often used a zero dollar threshold. For example, all four of the depository institutions we spoke with said they were already using a zero dollar threshold as part of their customer identification and recordkeeping practices. Also, in FinCEN's studies of the 2010 proposed rule, FinCEN determined that banks, by and large, keep records for funds transfers regardless of dollar value.

Nearly all of the money transmitters we interviewed also said that they already had self-imposed thresholds of around $1,000 for verifying and collecting information on funds transfers, and that most of their transactions were significantly below the $3,000 funds transfer threshold. The $1,000 threshold is an industry and international standard recommended by the Financial Action Task Force and, according to FinCEN in the 2010 proposed rule, adopted by many countries, which money transmitters must follow when operating in their jurisdictions. Some states have also implemented a recordkeeping threshold below the federal requirement that money transmitters in those states must comply with. For example, Arizona and Oklahoma have implemented a $1,000 threshold for recording certain information, including some identifying information.[100]

In the 2010 proposed rule, FinCEN stated that through extensive consultation with the industry, the threshold for money transmitters to report on international transfers of $1,000 or more was appropriate because the industry in large part already observed this threshold. Money transmitters we spoke with or stakeholders that commented on the 2006 advance notice generally did not advocate reducing the threshold for money transmitters to zero dollars, noting that eliminating the funds transfer threshold would be burdensome for them and would likely drive transactions underground. Similarly, law enforcement officials from DHS, DOJ, and IRS indicated that they did not support reducing the threshold to zero for money transmitters because doing so could impede legitimate transactions and cause remitters to resort to alternative methods of laundering proceeds. DHS officials noted that they would still have the authority to investigate alternative remittance systems.

Some stakeholders had concerns about a lower threshold, however, largely because of the additional recordkeeping and costs that would be involved. Some of these stakeholders also indicated that information already collected was sufficient, and that the additional cost to monitor the information at a lower amount would not be worth the benefits of law enforcement tracking such small amounts. Federal and state banking regulators we spoke with generally did not advocate for a lower funds transfer threshold. Officials from these regulators believed that reducing the threshold would require increased recordkeeping for banks, and one state regulator believed that it could increase costs for both providers and regulators which would need to review more transactions. In our review of the published comments to FinCEN's 2006 advance notice we found that nearly half (12 of the 25 commenters) recommended no change in the threshold largely because of the additional recordkeeping and costs involved. The comments opposed to lowering the threshold were mostly from or referred to relatively small community banks or credit unions that were opposed to the additional recordkeeping, in part because they were not already collecting and maintaining information for transactions below the federal threshold. Some of these commenters noted that additional recordkeeping and verification requirements would increase costs that would be passed on to customers, who then might turn to alternate forms of transmitting money.

Most Stakeholders Raised Concerns That Requirements to Verify Legal Immigration Status Would Increase the Use of Less Detectable Forms of Remittances

Most parties we spoke with, including officials from law enforcement, money transmitters, depository institutions, industry associations, and policy and consumer advocacy groups, voiced concerns about the implications of requiring verification of legal immigration status of remittance senders. Law enforcement officials we spoke with told us that a requirement to verify legal immigration status might not assist AML efforts and could lead senders to use less detectable forms of transmitting money, as the following examples illustrate.

- IRS officials said that the Remittance Status Verification Act would, if passed, effectively require an identification verification threshold of near zero and the collection of information on de minimis, or very minor, transaction amounts.[101] IRS concluded that verifying identities and collecting information at a near zero dollar threshold would not be useful and could cause remitters to resort to off-the-book methods.
- DHS officials we spoke with said that, in general, collecting identification information would be beneficial to investigations but that verifying legal immigration status would not necessarily hurt or help their investigations. They added that a lower funds transfer threshold was more crucial to their investigations. DHS officials did say that knowing senders' legal immigration status could be beneficial if DHS was looking at potentially removing illegal immigrants from the country. But they added that the verification requirements could drive remitters to informal remittance systems. One official noted that although criminals could turn to alternative methods of transferring money to avoid being identified, it could take several years to establish a new criminal financial network, and could result in a positive AML effect for a time—at least until the criminals identified alternative networks.

In interviews with us, officials from the five money transmitters, four depository institutions, six of their respective industry associations, and three policy and consumer advocacy groups nearly all raised concerns about asking for information from remittance senders about their legal immigration status in the United States. Among other things, they said doing so would likely contribute to pushing remittances out of formal financial systems to less detectable methods. Officials from two money transmitters we spoke with compared the potential outcomes to those they observed when the state of Oklahoma imposed a requirement they felt had similar implications.[102] According to these officials, the enactment of the Oklahoma legislation led to a significant drop of around 28 percent in their Oklahoma remittances shortly after the law was passed. However, an official from one of these money transmitters stated that the volume of transfers in surrounding states increased by as much as half during the same time period—indicating that some customers went to bordering states to conduct remittances to avoid the fee in Oklahoma. An official from the Oklahoma Bureau of Narcotics & Dangerous Drugs Control stated that he believed that the Oklahoma remittance fee had helped reduce transfers of proceeds from illicit activity from Oklahoma, adding that the amount collected annually in wire transmitter fees had increased.[103]

AGENCY COMMENTS AND OUR EVALUATION

We provided a draft of this report to CFPB, DHS, DOJ, Federal Reserve, FDIC, FTC, IRS, NCUA, OCC, Treasury, and USPS for review and comment. Officials from DHS, Federal Reserve, FDIC, OCC, and Treasury provided technical comments, which we incorporated as appropriate. CFPB, DOJ, FTC, and IRS had no comments on the report. In its letter, USPS said that they had no comments. In its letter, NCUA noted that the scale and scope of international remittances raise significant public policy issues, and that this report will go far toward informing the debate about constructive remittance policy.

Lawrance L. Evans, Jr.
Director, Financial Markets and Community Investment

APPENDIX I: OBJECTIVES, SCOPE, AND METHODOLOGY

Our objectives were to examine (1) the Bank Secrecy Act (BSA) remittance requirements that exist for remittance providers and related challenges that remittance providers face in complying with these requirements; (2) the money laundering risks that remittance transfer methods pose; (3) stakeholders' views on the extent to which requiring remittance providers to verify identification and collect information at a lower dollar transaction amount than is currently required, or adding a requirement to verify legal immigration status, would assist federal agencies' anti-money laundering (AML) efforts.[1]

To examine BSA remittance requirements for remittance providers, we reviewed relevant laws and regulations and obtained information from remittance providers on their efforts to comply with BSA (including their methods and practices) and the challenges they faced in these efforts. We also obtained and analyzed available data on money transmitters' compliance with BSA-related requirements. Compliance data we reviewed included Internal Revenue Service (IRS) BSA-related violation and exam data on money transmitters for fiscal years 2013 and 2014. We assessed the reliability of data provided to us by IRS by reviewing related documentation of the database from which the data come and also through interviews with agency officials, and found the data to be reliable for purposes of this report.

To examine the money laundering risks posed by remittance transfers, we reviewed and summarized available reports and documents that the Financial Crimes Enforcement Network (FinCEN), federal law enforcement, regulatory agencies, international organizations, and remittance providers maintained on money laundering through remittance transfers. We also collected and reviewed information from the Department of Justice (DOJ) and Department of Homeland Security (DHS) on closed money laundering cases from fiscal year 2006 to April 2015 involving remittance providers.

We also reviewed FinCEN data on the number of suspicious activity reports filed by money transmitters related to remittance transfers to determine the most frequently reported categories of suspicious activity. FinCEN noted that there were some limitations regarding the data on suspicious activity report filings related to international remittances. The totals of suspicious activities reported could exceed the actual number of reports filed because some reports can reflect more than one type of suspicious activity. For example, a single suspicious activity report may be counted in "Money Laundering" and "Structuring" because both categories in that report were selected. The data we reviewed were based on the number of money transmitters that selected "funds transfer" when reporting the type of payment mechanism involved in the suspicious activity; however, the statistics are incomplete because some filers (about 40 percent) did not fill out the payment mechanism. Additionally, the data are incomplete because the filers may not have filled out relevant fields that would identify whether a transfer was a remittance. We assessed the reliability of suspicious activity report data through interviews with agency officials and comparing information to published data. Although FinCEN noted limitations with the data, we found the data to be reliable for purposes of reporting the top two categories of suspicious activity filed by remittance providers, which were consistent with common methods of money laundering identified in the Department of the Treasury's 2015 *National Money Laundering Risk Assessment*.

For purposes of our report, stakeholders included officials from 30 entities: FinCEN, federal law enforcement entities—including representatives from a High Intensity Financial Crime Area, federal and state regulators, industry associations, money transmitters, depository institutions, and policy and consumer advocacy groups. To examine stakeholders' views on the extent to which lowering the funds transfer threshold for complying with recordkeeping requirements or adding a legal immigration status verification requirement would assist agencies' AML efforts we reviewed an advance notice of proposed rulemaking, a proposed rule, and proposed legislation related to remittance transfers— including 25 public comment letters available on the advance notice and proposed rule. We also obtained, through interviews, the views of stakeholders on the extent to which lowering the funds transfer threshold or adding a legal immigration status verification requirement (which could include requiring certain identification for transfers at the near zero dollar threshold) would further AML efforts. We researched and reviewed information on international customer identification standards for remittance transfers. Sources for this information included, among others: the Financial Action Task Force report, *International Standards on Combating Money Laundering and the Financing of Terrorism and Proliferation: The Financial Action Task Force Recommendations* (February 2012); the Financial Action Task Force, *Money Laundering through Money Remittance and Currency Exchange Providers* (June 2010); Department of State report, *Country Reports on Terrorism 2013*; FinCEN's report, *Feasibility of a Cross Border Electronic Funds Transfer System under the Bank Secrecy Act*; and PricewaterhouseCoopers, *Anti Money Laundering – Know Your Customer Quick Reference Guide* (January 2014).

For all objectives, we interviewed officials from FinCEN and federal law enforcement entities—including DHS, DOJ, and DHS representatives from the Southwest High Intensity Financial Crime Area. We also interviewed federal banking regulators and officials from the Conference of State Banking Supervisors, which included representatives from state banking regulators. In addition, we interviewed agency officials at the Consumer Financial and Protection Bureau and the Federal Trade Commission. We interviewed officials from depository institution industry associations including the American Bankers Association, The Clearing House, and Independent Community Bankers of America. We also interviewed money transmitter industry associations including The Money Services Roundtable, The National Money Transmitters Association, and the Association of Certified Anti-Money Laundering Specialists— representing both money transmitters and depository institutions. Additionally, we interviewed representatives from a policy group, Inter-American Dialogue, and two consumer advocacy groups—National Council of La Raza and Appleseed. Furthermore, we interviewed a selection of money transmitters and depository institutions. We judgmentally selected a cross-section of medium and large money transmitters and depository institutions that included five nondepository money transmitters and four depository institutions (two banks and two credit unions) based on a number of factors, including the volume of remittances and diversity of countries serviced. For all objectives, we also reviewed reports and guidance published by FinCEN and international organizations such as the World Bank and the Financial Action Task Force.

We conducted this performance audit from October 2014 to December 2015 in accordance with generally accepted government auditing standards. Those standards require that we plan and perform the audit to obtain sufficient, appropriate evidence to provide a reasonable basis for our findings and conclusions based on our audit objectives. We believe that the evidence obtained provides a reasonable basis for our findings and conclusions based on our audit objectives.

APPENDIX II: IRS BANK SECRECY ACT EXAMINATIONS OF MONEY TRANSMITTERS

Table 1. Summary of IRS Bank Secrecy Act Examinations of Money Transmitters, Fiscal Years 2013-2014

	Fiscal year 2014	Fiscal year 2013
Number of exams	**2,729**	**3,073**
Number of violations	**6,104**	**8,659**
Top 3 most frequently occurring violations:		
AML program requirements[a]	3,191	3,554
Reports of suspicious activity[b]	1,323	2,893
Recordkeeping—funds transfers[c]	531	838

Source: IRS data and GAO analysis. | GAO-16-65

[a]AML Compliance Program Violations 1022_210, 1022_210(d)(1), 1022_210(d)(2), 1022_210(d)(3), 1022_210(d)(4). These subcategory violations are all requirements for maintaining an adequate AML program. Subcategories include policies, procedures, and internal controls; designation of compliance officer; training; and independent review, respectively.

[b]Reporting violations 1022_320(a), 1022_320(b), 1022_320(c) . Money transmitters are required to file reports of any suspicious transaction relevant to a possible violation of law or regulation. 31 C.F.R. § 1022.320.

[c]Recordkeeping violation 1010_410(e). Money transmitters are required to obtain and retain specific information, such as the name and address of the sender, for each transfer of $3,000 or more. 31 C.F.R. § 1010.410(e).

Under delegated authority from the Financial Crimes Enforcement Network (FinCEN), the Internal Revenue Service (IRS) examines nondepository financial institutions—including money transmitters—for compliance with the Bank Secrecy Act (BSA).[1] According to IRS data, the results of examinations of money transmitters from fiscal years 2013 and 2014 showed that the top three most frequently cited violations were failure to comply with AML program requirements, failure to file suspicious activity reports, and inadequate recordkeeping of funds transfers.

End Notes

[1] World Bank Group, "Remittances growth to slow sharply in 2015, as Europe and Russia stay weak; pick up expected next year," (Apr. 13, 2015). We have ongoing work underway that will be reporting on the reliability of remittance estimates in a separate report that we plan to issue in fiscal year 2016.

[2] Definitions of remittances vary based on the transfer method, purpose, and provider—that is, the entity transferring the funds for the sender. For purposes of this report, we define remittances as the transfer of funds from consumers in the United States to persons or businesses in a foreign country.

[3] Financial Action Task Force, *Money Laundering through Money Remittance and Currency Exchange Providers* (June 2010), 7.

[4] Bank Secrecy Act, titles I and II of Pub. L. No. 91-508, 84 Stat. 1114 (1970) (codified as amended at 12 U.S.C. §§ 1829b, 1951-1959, and 31 U.S.C. § 5311 et seq.).

[5] 31 C.F.R. § 1020.410(a) (recordkeeping requirements for banks); 31 C.F.R. § 1010.410(e) (recordkeeping requirements for nondepository financial institutions). For simplification purposes we use the term "funds transfer" for both depository and nondepository institutions in this report. Under the BSA, the term "funds transfer" is used in the context of depository institutions, and the term "transmittal of funds"—which includes funds transfers—is used in the context of nondepository financial institutions. *See* 31 C.F.R. §§ 1010.100(w), (ddd), 1010.410(e), 1020.410(a).

[6] *See* Threshold for the Requirement to Collect, Retain, and Transmit Information on Funds Transfers and Transmittals of Funds, Advance Notice of Proposed Rulemaking, 71 Fed. Reg. 35,564 (June 21, 2006). The 2006 advance notice of proposed rulemaking was published jointly with the Board of Governors of the Federal Reserve System (Federal Reserve). *See also* Cross-Border Electronic Transmittals of Funds, Notice of Proposed Rulemaking, 75 Fed. Reg. 60,377 (Sept. 30, 2010).

[7] Remittance Status Verification Act of 2015, S. 79, 114th Cong. (2015). The Remittance Status Verification Act would amend the Electronic Fund Transfer Act, which provides a consumer protection framework for remittance transfers made by senders in the United States to recipients in a foreign country. The Electronic Fund Transfer Act defines a "remittance transfer provider" as "any person or financial institution that provides remittance transfers for a consumer in the normal course of its business, whether or not the consumer holds an account with such person or financial institution." 15 U.S.C. § 1693o-1(g)(3). The Electronic Fund Transfer Act defines a "remittance transfer" as the "electronic

transfer of funds requested by a sender located in any state to a designated recipient that is initiated by a remittance transfer provider, whether or not the sender holds an account with the remittance transfer provider," but does not include small value transactions in the amount of $15 or less. 15 U.S.C. § 1693o-1(g)(2); 12 C.F.R. § 1005.30(e).

[8] We obtained stakeholder views on both (1) lowering or eliminating the reporting dollar threshold for collecting and retaining information on funds transfers and (2) imposing a requirement that individuals document immigration status for funds transfers beginning at a near-zero threshold. Because imposing these requirements beginning at a low dollar threshold may result in similar challenges and benefits for law enforcement, stakeholders' views on a lower dollar threshold for required BSA recordkeeping may inform our discussion of the potential effects of the immigrant status documentation requirement. We will be considering the potential effects of imposing a fine on remittance senders unable to show proof of legal immigration status in greater depth in a separate report.

[9] The ACH is a system that clears and settles batched electronic transfers for participating depository institutions. International ACH makes up a small but growing portion of remittance transfers.

[10] Department of the Treasury, *2015 National Money Laundering Risk Assessment* (Washington, D.C.).

[11] 31 C.F.R. § 1010.100(ff).

[12] FinCEN regulations define a money transmitter as a person that provides money transmission services, which means the acceptance of currency, funds, or other value that substitutes for currency from one person and the transmission of currency, funds, or other value that substitutes for currency to another person or location by any means. The definition of money transmitter also includes any other person engaged in the transfer of funds. 31 C.F.R. § 1010.100(ff)(5). For purposes of this report, we focus on the money transmitter subset of money services businesses, and thus use the term "money transmitter" rather than "money services business" throughout the report. Money transmitters generally provide funds transfers, including international remittances, which are the focus of this report.

[13] Although USPS is treated as a separate subset of money services businesses from money transmitters under FinCEN regulations, we use the term "money transmitter" as including traditional money transmitters as well as USPS for the purposes of this report because USPS provides some comparable services to those money transmitters provide.

[14] Each money services business is generally required to register with FinCEN, and include in its registration, among other things, a list of its agents. *See* 31 C.F.R. § 1022.380(a).

[15] A money services business enters into a service agreement with the agent. Many of the terms of the agreement are generally stipulated by the state requirements where the money services business is located. Among other features, the agreement typically identifies the rights and obligations of both parties, as well as responsibilities for complying with all state and federal laws. In this report, the term "agent" does not denote a particular legal relationship. It includes legal agents, authorized delegates, or affiliates that act on behalf of a money transmitter in some capacity. Financial Crimes Enforcement Network and Internal Revenue Service, *Bank Secrecy Act/Anti-Money Laundering Examination Manual for Money Services Businesses* (December 2008).

[16] Money transmitters often instruct agents to pay out funds before the funds are sent to the foreign location. Money may be disbursed to the recipient in U.S. dollars or local currency depending on the destination, the money transmitter's service offering, and the preference of either the sender or the recipient.

[17] The financial industry commonly uses many terms to describe these additional financial institutions. These terms include "intermediary" financial institution, "instructing" financial institution, "sender's correspondent," and "receiver's correspondent." For purposes of this study, we use the term "correspondent" to describe these additional financial institutions. Financial Crimes Enforcement Network, *Feasibility of a Cross-Border Electronic Funds Transfer Reporting System under the Bank Secrecy Act* (October 2006).

[18] Consumer Financial Protection Bureau, *Report on Remittance Transfers* (July 20, 2011).

[19] *See* 79 Fed. Reg. 5302, 5306-07 n.37 (Jan. 31, 2014).

[20] Data for depository institution international money transfers were derived from calendar year 2014 call-report data reported by banks and credit unions on the number of remittance transfers originated.

[21] *See* 79 Fed. Reg. 55,970, 55,972 (Sept. 18, 2014).

[22] *See* 79 Fed. Reg. 5302, 5314 n.85 (Jan. 31, 2014).

[23] World Bank Group, "Remittances growth to slow sharply in 2015, as Europe and Russia stay weak; pick up expected next year," (Apr. 13, 2015).

[24] Each person (including a bank) who physically transports, mails, or ships currency or monetary instruments in excess of $10,000 at one time out of or into the United States (and each person who causes the transfer) must file a Report of International Transportation of Currency or Monetary Instruments (FinCEN Form 105). *See* 31 U.S.C. § 5316.

[25] Financial Crimes Enforcement Network in cooperation with INTERPOL/FOPAC, *The Hawala Alternative Remittance System and its Role in Money Laundering (January 2000).*

[26] 31 U.S.C. § 5330; 31 C.F.R. § 1022.380.

[27] As part of the process for obtaining a charter from a federal or state chartering authority, a depository institution typically provides information about its structure and ownership, as well as financial and managerial information and plans for compliance with applicable laws, including the BSA.

[28] For the purposes of this report, we use "federal banking regulators" to refer collectively to the regulators of depository institutions (federally insured banks, thrifts, and credit unions). Federal banking regulators include the Office of the Comptroller of the Currency (OCC), Federal Reserve, Federal Deposit Insurance Corporation (FDIC), and National Credit Union Administration (NCUA). Although CFPB has supervisory and enforcement authority over federal consumer financial law for certain entities, including large banks and certain nondepository institutions, we did not include CFPB in our definition of federal banking regulators because CFPB does not examine for compliance with or enforce BSA. *See* 12 U.S.C. §§ 5514, 5515.

[29] The appropriate federal prudential regulators are required to prescribe regulations requiring the insured depository institutions under their supervision to establish and maintain procedures that are reasonably designed to assure and monitor the compliance of such institutions with the BSA. 12 U.S.C. §§ 1786(q), 1818(s). Regulations requiring the establishment of BSA compliance programs are codified at 12 C.F.R. § 21.21 (OCC); 12 C.F.R. § 208.63 (Federal Reserve); 12 C.F.R. §§ 326.8, 390.354 (FDIC); 12 C.F.R. § 748.2 (NCUA).

[30] *See* 31 C.F.R. § 1010.810(b)(6),(9).

[31] Certain entities are specifically excluded from IRS's examination authority, including brokers or dealers in securities, mutual funds, futures commission merchants, introducing brokers in commodities, and commodity trading advisors. 31 C.F.R. § 1010.810(b)(8). As noted above, those entities are subject to examination by SEC and CFTC.

[32] FFIEC is a formal interagency body empowered to prescribe uniform principles, standards, and report forms for the federal examination of financial institutions by its member agencies and

to make recommendations to promote uniformity in the supervision of financial institutions. The constituent agencies are the Federal Reserve, Federal Deposit Insurance Corporation, National Credit Union Administration, Office of the Comptroller of the Currency, Bureau of Consumer Financial Protection, and State Liaison Committee, which consists of five representatives from state regulatory agencies that supervise financial institutions.

[33] Federal Financial Institutions Examination Council, *Bank Secrecy Act/ Anti-Money Laundering Examination Manual* (2014).

[34] Federal and state banking regulators conduct safety and soundness examinations of depository institutions. State regulators may examine depository institutions chartered within their jurisdiction. State regulators may also conduct safety and soundness examinations of nondepository financial institutions, such as money transmitters. The authority of states to regulate money transmitters varies from state to state.

[35] GAO, *Bank Secrecy Act: Opportunities Exist for FinCEN and the Banking Regulators to Further Strengthen the Framework for Consistent BSA Oversight*, GAO-06-386 (Washington, D.C.: Apr. 28, 2006), 5.

[36] 31 U.S.C. §§ 5320, 5321; 31 C.F.R. § 1010.810(a),(d). See 31 U.S.C. § 310; 67 Treasury Order 180-01, Fed. Reg. 64,697 (Sept. 26, 2002) for the source of FinCEN's overall enforcement and compliance authority.

[37] *See* 12 U.S.C. §§ 1786(b), (q) (federally insured credit unions), 1818(b), (c), (s) (depository institutions other than credit unions).

[38] *See* 12 U.S.C. §§ 1786(k)(2) (federally insured credit unions), 1818(i) (depository institutions other than credit unions).

[39] 31 C.F.R. § 1010.810(b)(8), (c)(2), (g). The authority to enforce certain provisions has been delegated from FinCEN to the Commissioner of Internal Revenue by means of a Memorandum Agreement between FinCEN and IRS, which provides that IRS has the authority to, among other things, assess and collect civil penalties under 31 U.S.C. § 5321 and 31 C.F.R. § 1010.810; investigate possible civil violations of these provisions; and issue administrative rulings under 31 C.F.R. pt. 1010, subpt. G. *See* 31 C.F.R. § 1010.810(g). IRS's Small Business/Self-Employed Division conducts BSA compliance examinations of money transmitters, and can refer cases to IRS Criminal Investigations if the examiners believe that a willful criminal violation may be involved. IRS Criminal Investigations investigate, among other types of criminal violations, BSA criminal violations.

[40] Remittance Status Verification Act of 2015, S. 79, 114th Cong. § 2 (2015).

[41] Okla. Stat. Ann. tit. 63, § 2-503.1j (West). Although this law does not require providers to verify legal immigration status of remitters, as noted, it imposes a fee on all remittances, regardless of remitters' legal status, and only those remitters who file income tax returns with the state may claim a credit for the fee paid. Since individuals who do not have proof of legal status are unlikely to have a valid Social Security number or tax identification number, they are unlikely to file income tax returns, and therefore unlikely to obtain a credit for the remittance fee paid. Legislation has been proposed in several other states that would impose a tax or fee on remittances with a later opportunity for a tax credit or refund—none of which have been enacted.

[42] H.B. 4120, 84th Leg., Reg. Sess. (Tex. 2015).The bill was left pending in committee as of April 2015.

[43] 31 U.S.C. § 5318(h)(1). For specific AML program requirements for money services businesses, including money transmitters, *see* 31 C.F.R. § 1022.210; for banks, *see* 31 C.F.R. § 1020.210.

[44] Financial Crimes Enforcement Network's guidance, *Frequently Asked Questions: Conducting Independent Reviews of Money Services Business Anti-Money Laundering Programs*, FIN-2006-G012, September 22, 2006, clarifies that, for a money transmitter, an independent review is not a formal audit by a certified public accountant or third-party consultant. Accordingly, a money services business does not necessarily need to hire an outside auditor or consultant. The review may be conducted by an officer, employee, or group of employees, so long as the reviewer is not the designated compliance officer and does not report directly to the compliance officer.

[45] Financial Crimes Enforcement Network, *Financial Institutions Outreach Initiative: Report on Outreach to Money Services Businesses* (July 2010).

[46] Specifically, a suspicious transaction is one that involves funds derived from illegal activity or is intended or conducted in order to hide or disguise funds or assets derived from illegal activity as part of a plan to evade any federal law or regulation, or any transaction reporting requirement under federal law or regulation. A suspicious transaction is also one that is designed, whether through structuring or other means, to evade any BSA requirements; one that serves no business or apparent lawful purpose and for which the reporting money transmitter knows of no reasonable explanation after examining the available facts; or one that involves use of the money transmitter to facilitate criminal activity. 31 C.F.R. § 1022.320(a)(2).

[47] A transaction is suspicious and requires reporting if it may involve potential money laundering or other illegal activity, is designed to evade the BSA or its implementing regulations, has no business or apparent lawful purpose or is not the type of transaction that the particular customer would normally be expected to engage in, and the institution knows of no reasonable explanation for the transaction after examining the available facts, including the background and possible purpose of the transaction. 31 C.F.R. § 1020.320(a)(2). Depository institutions are also required to file suspicious activity reports for criminal violations involving insider abuse of any amount, as well as violations aggregating $5,000 or more when a suspect can be identified and $25,000 or more even without a potential suspect. *See* 12 C.F.R. §§ 21.11(c)(1)-(3), 163.180(d)(3)(i)-(iii) (OCC); 12 C.F.R. § 208.62(c)(1)-(3) (Federal Reserve); 12 C.F.R. § 353.3(a)(1)-(3) (FDIC); 12 C.F.R. § 748.1(c)(1)(i)-(iii) (NCUA).

[48] Financial Crimes Enforcement Network, *SAR Stats Technical Bulletin* (October 2015).

[49] 31 C.F.R. § 1020.410(a) (recordkeeping requirements for banks); 31 C.F.R. § 1010.410(e) (recordkeeping requirements for nonbank financial institutions).

[50] 31 C.F.R. § 1010.410(f).

[51] 31 C.F.R. §§ 1010.410(e)(2), 1020.410(a)(2).

[52] An alien number is issued to noncitizens by U.S. Citizenship and Immigration Services. The alien identification number can be found on the permanent residence card, which gives the holder a way of proving his or her legal status to live and work permanently within the United States.

[53] 31 C.F.R. § 1020.220(a)(2).

[54] The preamble to the customer identification program final rule provides that the term "account" was limited to formal banking and business relationships established to provide "ongoing" services, dealings, or other financial transactions to make clear that this term is not intended to cover infrequent transactions such as the occasional purchase of a money order or a wire transfer. 68 Fed. Reg. 25,092, 25,092 (May 9, 2003). As a result, not all bank remittances transactions fall within the requirements of the customer identification program rule. According to OCC, most banks only permit "customers" with "accounts" to engage in

remittance transfers; however, some do not and the customer identification program may not apply to these situations when a non-customer is permitted to engage in remittance transfers.

[55] Financial Crimes Enforcement Network, *Financial Institutions Outreach Initiative: Report on Outreach to Money Services Businesses* (July 2010).

[56] A person who is a money transmitter solely because that person serves as an agent of another money services business (such as a money transmitter) is generally not required to register with FinCEN. 31 C.F.R. § 1022.380(a)(3). However, these agents are required to establish AML programs and comply with other recordkeeping and reporting requirements. See 31 C.F.R. § 1022.210(d)(1)(iii).

[57] In determining how much, if any, further due diligence is required for a money transmitter customer, depository institutions should consider the types of products and services the money transmitter offers, the location(s) and the market(s) it serves, anticipated account activity, and the purpose of the account. Financial Crimes Enforcement Network, Board of Governors of the Federal Reserve System, Federal Deposit Insurance Corporation, National Credit Union Administration, Office of the Comptroller of the Currency, Office of Thrift Supervision, *Interagency Interpretive Guidance on Providing Banking Services to Money Services Businesses Operating in the United States* (April 2005). The Office of Thrift Supervision was abolished in 2010 by the Dodd-Frank Act. Pub. L. No. 111-203, § 313, 124 Stat. 1376, 1523 (codified at 12 U.S.C. § 5413).

[58] 31 U.S.C. § 5318(g)(2).

[59] There is an exception for when the disclosure is requested by FinCEN, bank supervisory agencies, or appropriate law enforcement agencies. Financial Crimes Enforcement Network, Board of Governors of the Federal Reserve System, Federal Deposit Insurance Corporation, National Credit Union Administration, Office of the Comptroller of the Currency, Office of Thrift Supervision, *Interagency Interpretive Guidance on Sharing Suspicious Activity Reports with Head Offices and Controlling Companies* (Jan. 20, 2006). The Office of Thrift Supervision was abolished in 2010 by the Dodd-Frank Act. Pub. L. No. 111-203, § 313, 124 Stat. 1376, 1523 (codified at 12 U.S.C. § 5413).*See also* 31 C.F.R. §§ 1020.320(e), 1022.320(d).

[60] Financial Crimes Enforcement Network, *Guidance on Sharing Suspicious Activity Reports by Depository Institutions with Certain U.S. Affiliates* (Nov. 23, 2010). For purposes of this guidance, "affiliate" of a depository institution means any company under common control with, or controlled by, that depository institution. "Under common control" means that another company (1) directly or indirectly or acting through one or more other persons owns, controls, or has the power to vote 25 percent or more of any class of the voting securities of the company and the depository institution; or (2) controls in any manner the election of a majority of the directors or trustees of the company and the depository institution. "Controlled by" means that the depository institution (1) directly or indirectly has the power to vote 25 percent or more of any class of the voting securities of the company; or (2) controls in any manner the election of a majority of the directors or trustees of the company. See, e.g., 12 U.S.C. § 1841(a)(2).

[61] 75 Fed. Reg. 75,593 (Dec. 3, 2010).

[62] 75 Fed. Reg. at 75,595.

[63] Derisking can be the result of various drivers, such as concerns about profitability, prudential requirements, anxiety after a global financial crisis, and reputational risk. Financial Action Task Force, *FATF clarifies risk-based approach: case-by-case, not wholesale de-risking,*

accessed November 2, 2015, http://www.fatfgafi.org/documents/documents/rba-and-de-risking.html.

[64] Financial Crimes Enforcement Network, Statement on Providing Banking Services to Money Services Businesses (Nov. 10, 2014). For example, in September 2013, a global bank announced that it ended accounts with some of their money transmitter accounts—including those sending remittances to Somalia—due to the concerns regarding the regulatory risk of financial crimes, including terrorist financing occurring through these accounts. Barclays, *Barclays statement on Money Services Businesses,* accessed September 15, 2015, http://www.newsroom.barclays.com/r/2728/barclays_statement_on_money_service_ busine.

[65] Federal Financial Institutions Examination Council, *Bank Secrecy Act/Anti-Money Laundering Examination Manual* (2014).

[66] Financial Crimes Enforcement Network, Statement on Providing Banking Services to Money Services Businesses (Nov. 10, 2014).

[67]Federal Deposit Insurance Corporation, *Statement on Providing Banking Services*, FIL5-2015 (Jan. 28, 2015). Remarks by Thomas J. Curry, Comptroller of the Currency, Before the Association of Certified Anti-money Laundering Specialists (Mar. 17, 2014).

[68] Survey respondents included, among others, representatives from both depository institutions and money transmitters.

[69] World Bank, *Fact Finding Summary from De-risking Surveys*: *Withdrawal from Correspondent Banking: Where, Why, and What to Do about It and Report on the G20 Survey on De-risking Activities in the Remittance Market* (Washington D.C.: November 2015). The *G20 Survey on De-risking Activities in the Remittance Market* noted that there was a low response rate from banks and money transmitters, but considered the data to be reflective of the market since they had responses from money transmitters that covered a substantial portion of market share of the remittance market.

[70] Remarks of Jennifer Shasky Calvery, Director, FinCEN, Securities Industry and Financial Markets Association, Anti-money Laundering and Financial Crimes Conference (Jan. 30, 2014).

[71] *In the Matter of Thomas E. Haider*, FinCEN Matter No. 2014-08 (Dec. 18, 2014).

[72] Financial Crimes Enforcement Network, *Advisory to U.S. Financial Institutions on Promoting a Culture of Compliance*, (Aug. 11, 2014), Remarks by Thomas J. Curry Comptroller of the Currency Before the Association of Certified Anti-Money Laundering Specialists (Mar. 17, 2014).

[73] Department of Justice, Deputy Attorney General, *Individual Accountability for Corporate Wrongdoing,* Memorandum for the Assistant Attorney General, Antitrust Division; Assistant Attorney General, Civil Division; Assistant Attorney General, Criminal Division; Assistant Attorney General, Environment and Natural Resources Division; Assistant Attorney General, National Security Division; Assistant Attorney General, Tax Division; Director, Federal Bureau of Investigation; Director, Executive Office for United States Trustees; All United States Attorneys (Washington D.C.: Sept. 9, 2015).

[74] Department of the Treasury, *2015 National Money Laundering Risk Assessment* (Washington, D.C.).

[75] Department of the Treasury, *2015 National Money Laundering Risk Assessment* (Washington, D.C.).

[76] These include the presence of offshore financial centers, a previous high-risk designation based on experience, and known money laundering risks as identified in the Department of State's annual International Narcotics Control Strategy Report. U.S. Department of State, *2015*

International Narcotics Control Strategy Report, Volume II: Money Laundering and Financial Crimes (March 2015).

[77] The Office of Foreign Assets Control within Treasury administers and enforces sanctions such as blocking assets or restricting trade against countries and groups of individuals, such as terrorists and narcotics traffickers. Beginning in 2000, Treasury and Justice designated certain areas as High Intensity Financial Crime Areas: Chicago, Illinois; Los Angeles, California; San Francisco, California; Miami, Florida; San Juan, Puerto Rico; the southwest border (Texas and Arizona); and New York and New Jersey. High Intensity Financial Crime Area designations were designed to allow law enforcement to concentrate resources in areas where money laundering or related financial crimes were occurring at a higher-than-average rate.

[78] Financial Crimes Enforcement Network, *Application of FinCEN's Regulations to Persons Administering, Exchanging, or Using Virtual Currencies Guidance,* FIN-2013-G001 (Mar. 13, 2013).

[79] Specifically, under BSA regulations, a person structures a transaction if that person, acting alone, or in conjunction with, on behalf of, other persons, conducts or attempts to conduct one or more transactions in currency, in any amount at one or more financial institutions, on one or more days, in any manner, for the purpose of evading specified reporting requirements. 31 C.F.R. § 1010.100(xx).

[80] *See* 31 U.S.C. § 5324, which prohibits structuring and imposes a criminal penalty.

[81] Department of the Treasury, *2015 National Money Laundering Risk Assessment* (Washington, D.C.).

[82] Data on suspicious activity report filings related to international remittances have some limitations. See appendix I for more information.

[83] United States Attorney's Office, Eastern District of New York, Twenty-Seven Individuals Charged in Continuing Probe of Drug Money Laundering in Money Remitter Industry, news release, February 7, 2007.

[84] Department of the Treasury, *2015 National Money Laundering Risk Assessment* (Washington D.C.).

[85] Department of the Treasury, *2015 National Money Laundering Risk Assessment* (Washington, D.C.).

[86] USA v. Wachovia Bank N.A., Deferred Prosecution Agreement, 10-20165-CR-Lenard, March 16, 2010; See also OCC, In the Matter of Wachovia Bank, National Association, Consent Order for a Civil Money Penalty, #2010-036, March 10, 2010. OCC found that Wachovia N.A. "failed to implement adequate policies, procedures, or monitoring controls governing the repatriation of nearly $14 billion of USD bulk cash for high risk casa de cambio and other foreign correspondent customers."

[87] *See* 8 U.S.C. § 1324.

[88] *See* Financial Crimes Enforcement Network, *Guidance on Recognizing Activity that May be Associated with Human Smuggling and Human Trafficking – Financial Red Flags*, FIN-2014-A008 (Sept. 11, 2014) (citing 18 U.S.C. §§ 1581, 1584, 1589, 1590, 1591, 2421, 2422, 2423, 2425; The Victims of Trafficking and Violence Protection Act of 2000, Pub. L. No. 106-386 (2000)).

[89] Department of the Treasury, *2015 National Money Laundering Risk Assessment* (Washington, D.C.).

[90] Financial Crimes Enforcement Network, *Guidance on Recognizing Activity that May be Associated with Human Smuggling and Human Trafficking – Financial Red Flags*, Advisory FIN-2014-A008 (Sept. 11, 2014).

[91] According to FinCEN, a funnel account is a bank account located in one geographic area that receives multiple deposits, often in amounts below the cash reporting threshold. Funds are often withdrawn from someone in a different geographic location with little time elapsing between deposits and withdrawals. *See* FinCEN (May 2014) Advisory FIN-2014- A005 for a detailed description of funnel accounts.

[92] Moneygram Deferred Prosecution Agreement, Statement of Facts, November 9, 2012.

[93] Federal Trade Commission, International Consumer Complaints, January – December 2014 (June 2015).

[94] Department of the Treasury, *2015 National Money Laundering Risk Assessment* (Washington, D.C.).

[95] Data on suspicious activity report filings related to international remittances have some limitations. See appendix I for more information.

[96] Financial Crimes Enforcement Network, Federal Reserve, Threshold for the Requirement to Collect, Retain, and Transmit Information on Funds Transfers and Transmittals of Funds, Joint Advance Notice of Proposed Rulemaking, 71 Fed. Reg. 35,564 (June 21, 2006). Several law enforcement agencies commented on this advance notice of proposed rulemaking.

[97] A DOJ official we interviewed said that the observations from this letter were generally still valid.

[98] Financial Crimes Enforcement Network, *Feasibility of a Cross-Border Electronic Funds Transfer Reporting System under the Bank Secrecy Act* (October 2006).

[99] Financial Crimes Enforcement Network, Cross-Border Electronic Transmittals of Funds, Notice of Proposed Rulemaking, 75 Fed. Reg. 60,377 (Sept. 30, 2010).

[100] *See* Ariz. Rev. Stat. Ann. § 6-1241(E); Okla. Admin. Code § 85:15-7-5.

[101] As discussed previously, the Remittance Status Verification Act would amend the Electronic Fund Transfer Act (EFTA), so the proposed law, if passed, would be subject to EFTA's definition of remittance transfer. 15 U.S.C. § 1693o-1(g)(2). Regulation E, which implements EFTA, excludes small value transactions of $15 or less from its definition of remittance transfer. 12 C.F.R. § 1005.30(e)(2)(i).

[102] As discussed previously, Oklahoma enacted a law in July 2009 requiring that a fee be imposed on all remittances that originate in Oklahoma. Although this law does not require providers to verify legal immigration status of remitters, it imposes a fee on all remittances, regardless of remitters' legal status, and only those remitters who file income tax returns with the state may claim a credit for the fee paid. Since individuals who do not have proof of legal status are unlikely to have a valid Social Security number or tax identification number, they are unlikely to file income tax returns, and therefore unlikely to obtain a credit for the remittance fee paid.

[103] For wire transmitter fee collections increasing in Oklahoma, see *Oklahoma Tax Commission, Annual Reports* (Oklahoma City, OK: June 30, 2011 through 2015). Also, there may be other economic factors contributing to the increase in Oklahoma wire transfer collections, including generally low remittance revenue during the recession from 2007 through 2009. See Suírez-Orozco, Marcelo M., *The Remittance Hole*, Americas Quarterly, vol. 3, no. 2 (Spring 2009), 85-89.

End Note for Appendix I

[1] We obtained stakeholder views on both (1) lowering or eliminating the reporting dollar threshold for collecting and retaining information on funds transfers and (2) imposition of a requirement that individuals document immigration status for funds transfers beginning at a near-zero threshold. Because imposing these requirements beginning at a low dollar threshold may result in similar challenges and benefits for law enforcement, stakeholders views on a lower dollar threshold for required BSA recordkeeping may inform our discussion of the potential effects of the immigrant status documentation requirement GAO has ongoing work underway that will be reporting on the reliability of remittance estimates in a separate report that it plans to issue in fiscal year 2016.

End Note for Appendix II

[1] *See* 31 C.F.R. § 1010.810(b)(8).

INDEX

E

F

G

H

I

W